KARLON L BROOKS

authorHOUSE

AuthorHouse™
1663 Liberty Drive
Bloomington, IN 47403
www.authorhouse.com
Phone: 1 (800) 839-8640

Published by AuthorHouse 11/14/2019

ISBN: 978-1-7283-3606-0 (sc)
ISBN: 978-1-7283-3604-6 (hc)
ISBN: 978-1-7283-3605-3 (e)

Print information available on the last page.

Any people depicted in stock imagery provided by Getty Images are models, and such images are being used for illustrative purposes only. Certain stock imagery © Getty Images.

This book is printed on acid-free paper.

Because of the dynamic nature of the Internet, any web addresses or links contained in this book may have changed since publication and may no longer be valid. The views expressed in this work are solely those of the author and do not necessarily reflect the views of the publisher, and the publisher hereby disclaims any responsibility for them.

This is a work of fiction. All of the characters, names, incidents, organizations, and dialogue in this novel are either the products of the author's imagination or are used fictitiously.

My. Vision

I wanted to express a vision that I see.

How we as African Americans can come together as a race and make good on the sacrifices of our ancestors. Often we read books, watch movies, or documentaries about the struggles and sacrifices of our ancestors. My Vision is to show how we can come together as other races have done. Not just in one community but across this nation. Not by fighting and killing each other but by working together, communicating. We have come a long way since the days of our ancestors. We have made great strides and progress. We now have millionaire sports stars, lawyers and judges, doctors and surgeons, real estate moguls and banking financiers, engineers and, chemical workers. Showing we can not only be equal but we can excel. It's time for us to show that not only can we make individual progress but we can come together, showing how we can be successful by showing strength in numbers, and with our minds and voices 0rather than fists

We have often criticized the fact that our money does l9not stay in our community. How that business

s suffer because they do not profit from money earned by the patrons of their own community. One way for black businesses to help each other is to do business with each other. One way I feel we can do this, is to have black businesses register to one place two allow other black businesses to know what goods and services they are selling or providing. Selling should not be restricted to black businesses however purchasing mainly from other black businesses is what will help our cause. We always encourage people to support black businesses, this method will allow us to know where those businesses are and what goods and services they are selling or providing. This is a means of keeping black money in the black community. There need not be any fees involved with this registration, all of this is done voluntarily, this is simply a matter of communication. This process need not be restricted to any particular community or city. The more widespread the communication goes the better for the businesses.

We as a people have the means to be self-sufficient. We have teachers, lawyers, doctors, skilled contractors, law enforcement specialist. We have the means to help ourselves. To teach the youths for our future. There are aplenty things we would like to do to improve our way of life and our standard of living. Of course the subject of financing will come into play and yes we will ask those of our well to do. Athletes, actors, celebrities looking for ways to give back to the community. There may already exist black owned financial institutions or the option of creating our own financial institution with the backing of our celebrities and such. A financial board can be created to make financial decisions on loans and such. Our people volunteering their knowledge or skills is key to our success. I have watched numerous movies and documentaries on our past, and how we came together by our people volunteering and sacrificing to overcome suppression. My thoughts are to put in writing the possibility of our future. So whether it be by book movie or documentary this is a look into our future, according to MY VISION.

After high school, working at a supermarket, singing with a group called, THE DEVASTATIONS Karlon thinks he is really doing something or going somewhere, living with mom and dad in HILL MANOR, Karlon's family life is well balanced, dad a postal worker for 20 yrs., mom with the board of education for 15yrs. Karlon's brother Ed, just out of college working 2 jobs, sis Karien in last year of high school. Karlon thinking he's got it all figured out. But on the upside he is working on getting his driver's license, putting away money each week, in a savings account suggested by mom, for a car.

Yea some of it actually worked out. He meets his girlfriend (Samira) from high school, got his license, and saved up enough money to get his first car, Oldsmobile Delta 88 1968,actually he brought it from a well known radio personality, Bill Franklin of WNJR.

Well the status stayed quo for a couple of years until whoops daisy his girlfriend Samira got pregnant. Ok now he has really got to do some real thinking. So he and Samira got an apartment together.

Thinking for the future Karlon decided to look for a part-time job. Karlon's older brother Ed works a part time job with a guy Bill. who owns a sandwich deli, so Ed got Karlon the hook up with Bill (a part time job).Karlon just had to work around his full time job at Foodtown. Karlon's singing group dates become less frequent.

As time goes on Karlon and Bill started a real good friendship, personal, business, and fun. Conversations began to lengthen with regularity, even bowling together on a team. Karlon began to do well working and learning the operations of the deli. So things start to get serious as the subject of karlon actually owning his own store came up. Bill wanting to expand his deli franchise and Karlon looking for financial security all seemed like a good idea. Karlon constantly looks for advice from Bill concerning owning his own store and getting a small business loan to do so.

Bill says to Karlon," I can get you a small business loan because my girlfriend works in a bank, and she may be able to push your loan through". But when it came to push and shove Karlon's credit was not good enough and Bill's girlfriend no longer worked at the bank. Now Karlon and Bills conversation start to include the difficulty of black owned businesses. Karlon begins to ask a question why Jews, Italians and Chinese are so successful in the black neighborhoods with business. Rather than the black owned businesses in their own neighborhood and being successful. Bill interjects, "blacks don't communicate with each other, they are too often in competition with each other rather than helping each other as the Chinese and Jews do "Chinese do business with other Chinese the Jews do business with other Jews in order to help each other's business grow. So now Karlon concluded that maybe black business owners don't know to help themselves or other black business owners because they don't know what other black business owners are out there for them to deal with. Karlon's idea now is to infuse this communication level with black owned businesses. In this day and age of computers and social media there is no excuse of this in his opinion. A website can be formed for black-owned businesses owners to join and register their businesses and what services they provide or products they sell. Karlon asked Bill, "how about setting up a website,"

Bill I don't know how to, but you can find out how, and there are online places that will do it for you, and some at no cost. So Karlon decides to sit down all night at a computer and build a website for that reason alone. Not being much of a computer whiz this is why it took him all night to do so. So being at the ground level and at the start-up of this website Bill and his Deli was the first to register at this website.

So now Bill starts to communicate with other black business owners in the community that he knows, and gets them onto the website. Companies such as a tool sharpening equipment company, a meat company, a bakery, and coincidentally Bill's brother also owns a deli. So as it goes each one informs all of his other black business contacts. And just like that the website registration begins to lengthen and more and more black business owners begin to register. So as the website becomes more popular, Karlon realizes that by widening this information across state lines would increase the popularity and communication level among black business owners. As time goes on this is exactly what happens many black owned businesses start to register as far as Los Angeles, Seattle, down to Houston. During this registration growth period the word of this website gets out to mainstream media. And whoops a daisy here come the problems.

Coming home from the store Karlon sees lights, news trucks, people, and police outside his building. So he says to himself oh crap somebody got shot or something, as he continues to proceed to his building someone draws attention to him by calling his name,

Reporter, "Karlon Brooks are you the owner of the black business website,"

Karlon, answers, "Well I started a website, I don't consider it mine, why are you asking, and who are you?"

Reporter, "Well my name is Guy Thomas and I work for Channel 13 News we were informed there is a website growing popularity with black business owners so I tracked you down as the owner."

So Karlon replies," so look you guys looking to interview me, you will have to wait till I consider what to tell you. Right now a group of businessmen are communicating on a website. Not much other than that."

Mr. Thomas reply, "you can call me, or come down to the station on Broad Street, when you are ready to be interviewed or add some facts about the website." Ok Karlon replies. Karlon goes into his apartment and immediately calls Bill on the phone. "Hey Bill do you know there were reporters outside my house asking me Questions about the website?"

Bill says," No really? What they want?" Karlon.says.".Asking me if I was the owner of the website, I said I started it but don't consider myself the owner." Bill says "Karlon well that kinda does mean you're the owner. What else did you tell them?"

Karlon replies "Nothing, I did not give them room for more questions." Karlon continues, "So look if this is going to be an issue in the media and public eye we need to consider where do we go from here and how to handle it."

Bill says "What do you mean we kemosabe?"

Karlon, "Well if that's the case, I don't want to be no dictator this website is for the benefit of black business owners, not me, I don't want anything to stop it or put in a negative light. Once it gets in the public eye people are going to be saying crap that ain't true, haters are going to try and knock it down, and whites that want to keep us down are going to try and shut it down.,

So what I'm going to do is email the business owners and propose a meeting."

Bill "What's that going to do?"

Karlon "Well I'm going to get a feel of what the owners want to do about possible scrutiny."

.Bill "What scrutiny? What could they say you have done wrong ".

Karlon "I don't know, but I want to be prepared for it. "You know how haters are going to bring stuff out they butts. So look I'll holla at you later, let me think on some stuff.

Bill," Ok kemosabe see you later."

Karlon again spends time to send out emails

Dear owners it has come to my attention that the media and other public interest have begun to question the website that we use for communication and business, I for one do not wish for the progress that we have made to stop, so I would like to get the feeling of all the owners to know what source of action we should take and how to address the media and public. So I propose that we have a meeting, not just for this course of action but also to organize ourselves to be prepared for later actions that may need to be taken. I am aware that all owners may not attend this meeting so any decisions that are made will be based on the amount of owners that are at the meeting. All others will be addressed and informed later.

Karlon places a call to Bill Karlon "Hey Bill I know you know about the website meeting, so I am wondering if we can use your catering hall next to your deli to have the meeting based on the number of owners that will attend. It will also give you the opportunity to show your business to the other owners and maybe use that as a form of advertisement to them"

Karlon gets up to the deli and catering hall early to meet some of the business owners as they come in to the meeting place. Slowly but surely the place begins to fill and Karlon is at the door meeting the owners and greeting them like a politician. Bill is on the other side in the deli giving instructions to his employees as he comes to the meeting hall to attend the meeting. Bill joins Karlon at the door and does the same greeting the owners. Bill does take this time to advertise his deli and catering hall by welcoming the owners to observe his deli while open for business and ask them to observe walk-in freezer to show how big they are and the storage he has in order to facilitate his catering business also providing hors d'oeuvres and refreshments on the side in the meeting hall. Karlon and Bill observe that the meeting Hall it's just about full and just as perfect as it can be the last person that comes in the door sits in the last open seat. Time to start the meeting. Bill picks up the mic "Hello ladies and gentlemen I'm Bill G welcome, this is my deli and catering operation. I'm here as a business owner as you are, if there are any questions regarding my store and catering please see me after the meeting, but as for the reason you are here you can ask this young man Karlon Brooks." As Karlon stands and takes the mic from Bill it gets a little noisy and clapping ensues before Karlon gets a word out everyone is standing and clapping.

The Meeting

Karlon, "Thank you everyone, welcome, I hope you are all clapping when you leave. The reason you are all here is to get answers to questions you may have to the operation and future of the website. Actually I got you all here so we can answer it together, as I am assuming by the turnout the website has done what I set it out to do, put black business owners in communication with each other. However I have bittersweet news for you all. Bad news first, no permanent decision will be made today. 241 members are here today, the good news is that that number represents less than half of our total membership." Again it gets a little noisy before the clapping starts." Thank you thank you thank you". Karlon says.

"So now for the meat of the matter, I want to let you know why I started the website it was a conversation with Bill G. that after a failed attempt to open my own business we discussed the difficult times of black business owners, and blacks helping blacks in business. Why is it that blacks don't get support from other black, one reason is because of the lack of knowing what other black businesses are out there. This website was designed to put a dent in that statistic. By the turnout here and by what our total numbers are, we may have started something." Immediately a clapping begin.

"It seems to me that you guys approve of the website and its purpose". Karlon says "but as I said I want us all to determine what steps we take for the future of the website. Due to the fact that the media is asking questions about the website is a question to me. I want us all to be on the same page as to what steps we take when such issues arrive. Why reporters want information on a website I do not know. What it is that they want to know about the website I do not know. But I wanted to bring this to all of you first before I did anything. A reporter from Channel 13 showed up at my home asking questions about the black website I did not give him anything cause as I said I want to discuss it with you. Personally if it was up to me I would not tell them anything because they are not members of this group which means it's none of their business what we do. So for now we can come up with a consensus as to what we want to do, and I will post it to the rest of the members online and we will make Communications that way from now on so you guys don't have to be coming back and forth traveling. So now I will open the floor to questions and suggestions I can only ask that you introduce yourself and your business to the group before speaking." A couple of people stand at one time but one raises his hand and speaks, "hello ladies and gentlemen

My Name is Earl Harris and I am the owner of a limousine company in Tampa Florida. My question to you Mr. Brooks, "and just as he says that

Karlon interrupts", no excuse me it's just Karlon Mr. Brooks makes me feel old, okay"

Mr. Harris responds," "that's fine, my question is are you the spokesman for this group? And how did that come about? Are we to choose a leader or spokesman or is this to be a foregone conclusion that this position belongs to you?"

"No sir "Karlon answers, "It is not a foregone conclusion at any time if you wish to start voting on positions I am for it, I'm only speaking because I was the one that put the website together and as I said the media approached me about it. At that time another person stood and spoke,

"Hello ladies and gentlemen my name is Dennis Jackson and I own a corner store in Trenton New Jersey and as far as I'm concerned and I'm pretty sure most of us feel this way that Mr. Brooks or Karlon should be the spokesman for this particular group until such time that we determine that he should not be." At that time again clapping begin and people began to stand and applaud.

Now Karlon says, "Okay, I'm going to take that as a vote let's go to the next question." A lady then stands and addresses the group, "Hello my name is Sylvia Banks, and I own a beauty supplies store in Boston Massachusetts my two questions are what is the name of this group? And actually how many members are there.

Karlon answers and says, "Actually the total count on membership is 516. And as for the name of the group, nothing is written in stone I only answered to the name that was first called to me as the black Business website. If there are any other suggestions you can suggest them on the website and we will have another thing to vote on. Personally I don't think that should be a name I think that that will only draw attention to us that we don't need. Remember we are just a group of people communicating with each other." Another gentleman stands and says,

"Hello ladies and gentlemen my name is John Hill I also own a deli in the Bronx New York my question is to Karlon what is it that you are gaining in this website group."

Karlon replies, "If you mean financial gain the answer is none. I do this purely because I want to see change in our people and I thought of a way that could happen so I wanted to suggest it to you as a group. Since the Inception of this website I believe that the website has benefited some of you or it would not be this many people here. Actually I am envisioning other possibilities coming about as a result of this website and our gathering, but that right now is for another time so if there are any more questions". Just as Karlon finishes speaking he notices to his right a police officer entering the meeting and walking towards the front. So Karlon steps to the side and ask the officer" can I help you sir is there something wrong Karlon asked?"

"Yes" the officer says, "the cars in the parking lot do they belong to your meeting members?

Karlon replies, "Yes, is there a problem?" Karlon asked "Actually yes" he replies, "We received a complaint from the parking lot owner about unauthorized cars in the parking lot. Also what is this meeting what's going on here?"

Karlon then replies, "Well sorry I actually don't believe that's true because the owner of the parking lot is right here to my left and I'm pretty sure he made no such calls. As to the subject of this meeting it's private so I do not believe the reason for our presence here needs to be made public so is that actually your reason for being here?"

The officer replies "I'm only following orders sir."

Karlon says, "Ok well I believe I answered your questions, is there anything else?" Just as that is said the officer turns and walks out. One of Bill's employees walks over to him and said

"Bill are you aware that there are police officers checking the license plates of the cars in the parking lot?"

Bill walks out to the parking lot to ask the officer" what seems to be the problem here why are you checking license plates? It seems to me that you are trying to start a problem. But from what I know what you will find is that most of these cars are car rentals because these people are from out of town".

The officer says, "I'm just following orders sir."

Two more members come out to the parking lot and ask Bill what seems to be the issue here.

Bill replies "I'm not sure, these guys are checking plates for some reason saying they are under orders to do so it sounds fishy to me something's going on here." One of the members walks to the officer, "officer what's going on here please tell me why you're doing what you're doing and who is giving you orders to do so?"

The officer replies, "I'm not sure I need to explain that to you I just talked to the gentleman that claims he is the owner of the parking lot". The member reaches in his pocket pulled out a wallet and badge and explains "I am a police officer of the state I wish to know your immediate supervisor, is it the desk sergeant or your captain? You know what never mind. I know who to call I'll find out what's going on here in 2 minutes."

Approximately 5 minutes later the officers get calls in their car radios and leave the scene. Bill and the member return inside.

Bill says to Karlon "I will tell you what happened outside after the meeting." So Karlon returns to address the group.

"I would like to return to the main purpose of our being here, how do you guys want to answer the following questions? Number one do we have a name or we going to name the website? Number two. Do we want to tell them what we are about, what we are doing?" A member stands and it says, "Yes. Again My Name is Earl Harris I don't know about everyone else but I feel the media can do us good. By advertising what we're doing when they report to the public. This is a way more owners can find out about the website. That can only do us good."

Karlon replies, "Yes I would have to agree with that point of view. That's like free advertisement. So what about the name? Are we going to use one or not?"

Bill stands and says "yes we should use a name, especially a name that draws attention." Karlon replies, "Well these are good ideas but as I said before there is not enough members here to make final decisions on things like that so we will suggest names on the website and we will go from there to give other members of the group a voice in this matter it's only fair that all members be heard." As to the website and its future Karlon says. "I still believe the website can grow and do even more for black businesses and the black community as a whole. So please keep spreading the word and doing good business with each other. Get more involved in your local communities Again I will say if there are any questions or suggestions, they can be asked now or if you come up with things later, post them on the web." A lady raised her hand and stood.

"My name is Linda Smith, I own a beauty shop in Harlem. You said there may be other benefits of the site, what did you mean by that?"

Karlon replies "Yea, I think that with the growth of our membership we may be able to help each other in multiple ways. Some of us have other professions, like Lawyers, doctors and such, so that maybe a plus, If others are looking to better the black community by ways of their professions this would be a way to expand the benefits of our communications on the website. If you are in a profession that one of our members need help with, help them out. Remember this is just a kick-start to us communicating with each other in order to help each other we need not have titles or specific positions. Communication cost nothing there's no specific laws we need to follow in order to communicate with each other. However I would like to say that no business transactions should be done on the website you guys can do business in your normal fashion, get telephone numbers email addresses, network with each other. No business transactions should be done on the website this is basically for your safety and to avoid possible law infractions and things of that nature. You may however advertise on the site in order to allow other members to know what you're doing as a business, and how you may be able to help other's businesses by doing so. So now I'm pretty much done as far as I'm concerned you guys can network amongst each other tour Bill's business. If you have questions for him you can do so. If anybody else wishes to come up and make any statements or questions you're welcome to do so. Enjoy the food and your time here. I'm still available for questions thank you." After that members start to mingle, eat, and tour Bill's kitchen. A lot of members actually take Bill's menus along with them. The meeting members begins to dissipate it begins to come clear that the meeting is over.

The Morning After

The morning after the meeting Bill G. arrived at the store to his store manager waiting for him.

"Jerome, what's up? You look like you want to say something".

"Yea!" he says … we got a summons this morning, it was on the door when I opened this morning sanitation … saying our garbage was not properly put out on the curb. It looks like our garbage was all over the ground

. Bill replies," Ok I will talk to Ali (the night mgmt.) to see what is what. So other than that. What's up for today?"

". Well Jerome replies we need to get some menus printed, looks like we got cleaned out last night."

Bill answers, "We have some in boxes on the shelf in back."

"Yea" Jerome says "But just one box, how long will that last?"

Bill, "Yea ok I will call for more meanwhile put them behind the register and give them out on request only."

"Ok" Jerome replies.

During the day bill received a call from his brother.

Randy "How did it go last night with the restaurant? Did you pick up any new customers from the meeting?"

Bill says "Not sure yet but a lot of menus were taken. So much that I have to order some earlier than usual. But a strange thing happened last night. Apparently my garbage cans were thrown about on the street and ground, seems like an animal may have gotten in them and as a result I got a summons for my garbage being on the ground."

Randy replies, "don't you have cans with the top lock on them so that doesn't happen."

Bill replies, "Yes I do that's why it's strange because this is something that doesn't usually happen. I will ask Ali to make sure that the cans at tops on them."

Randy says, "Don't you also have a camera in the back where you can see the street to see if animals got to your garbage."

Bill replied "yes I do I did not think of that, going to check that soon as I hang up from you."

Randy says, "Don't wait do it now I'll talk to you later."

Bill calls Jerome into the office, "Hey dude roll up the camera from last night. Let's see what happened to the garbage cans last night or this morning. Not even going to wait until Ali comes in."

So Bill and Jerome sit down and watch the tape from the camera, starting last night after closing till morning time, as the tape goes on

Bill says, "That it seems nothing happened last night so let's check in the morning. Jerome fast forward that tape until he sees a police car come in front of the garbage area, as the police car comes in front of the garbage the door opens so that it hits the garbage cans and knocks them over on the ground, once this is done the door closes and the police car leaves the scene.

Jerome says, "To Bill I don't believe I just saw that." and Bill says to Jerome "I'm glad you saw it so that I'm not the only one." Just as they are talking, the camera is still rolling and another police car comes about and stops and officer gets out and writes the summons and places it on the door.

Bill's eyes open wide and he yells, "That's the cop that came into the meeting! What the hell is his problem?" Bill leans back in the chair and says "Okay. We officially have a problem. So I need to make some calls to see how to deal with this. No need to talk to Ali." Randy calls Bill's Restaurant just after they saw the camera tapes. But Karlon answers the phone,

Karlon says, "Hey Randy Bill left out, interesting night last night huh.

Randy asked" how did you guys dof?" At this moment and time

Karlon says "Interesting. It's not the word for last night period, we had some issues with the police outside last night looking at cars and now I see on the camera that a police car knocked over our garbage cans on purpose and then gave us a ticket for the garbage being on the ground. And this is the same cop that came into the meeting asking questions, wanting to know what the meeting was about."

Karlon laughed "It's just crazy."

Randy asked "What are you going to do about it?"

Karlon replies, "Don't know yet."

Randy says, "Tell Bill to call me when he returns."

A couple of hours later after Bill returns he gets a call.

Mr. G "Hello my name is Joyce Brown I was at the meeting last night. I think what you and Karlon are doing is a great and a needed thing."

Bill replied, "Thank you Miss Brown but I cannot take credit for that. This Enterprise, as far as the website is concerned, it's a product of Karlon Brooks, would you like me to give you a number for him? Well no Miss Brown says," Although I realize your brother also has a deli my reason for calling is for your catering operation, I would like to explore your prices for doing a wedding. My apologies Miss Brown you have to forgive me my head is not on straight this morning I need to start looking for a new lawyer my garbage was purposely knocked over by the police last night.

Miss Brown replied "Wow Mr. G. You said a new lawyer, what happened with your previous lawyer?"

Bill replies, "Actually my lawyer passed".

Ms. Brown says," Wow sorry to hear that but maybe you should have talked to more of your guest last night, one of them was a lawyer. I remember having a conversation with a Mr. Simmons who owns and operates a home improvement company is also a lawyer."

"Wow thanks Miss Brown, Bill replied I will look him up in the membership roll, as for your wedding prices I'm going to have you talk to my store manager Jerome and he can give you all the prices and hook you up with all that we provide for weddings. But just to let you know I am considering a discount for website members.

Bill calls Mr. Simmons, "Hello Mr. Simmons this is Bill. G you were at the meeting last night. I understand that you are a lawyer. And I have an issue that I believe I need a lawyer to look into, what is your availability."

Mr. Simmons replies," a really nice event last night I really like your store and the subject of the meeting. I did not get a chance to talk to you personally but you and Mr. Brooks seem to have things going well, as far as the website is concerned. Is this why you need a lawyer?

Bill replies," 1no I have an issue at my store. the police department is harassing me, I would like to give you more detail but there is something that you need to see in person so let's arrange a time when you can come to the store according to your availability." okay Mr. Bill Mr. Simmons Says "let me look at my book and I will get back to you as soon as I can, I promise it will not be longer than one day." After this conversation Bill called Randy,

"hey Randy I looked at the videos and you will not believe what we saw. I am apparently being harassed by the police department, I don't know why but I just talked to a lawyer about the police purposely knocking over my garbage cans and writing me a ticket. Once the lawyer sees the video he will decide what action to take. I am not placing blame on anyone but it seems to be related to the meeting for some reason or another."

In The Public Eye

After announcing to the membership about going public Karlon seeks out a reporter that was at his home looking to get info on the website. So he goes to the station of channel 13. Just as he approached the front desk, someone calls, "Mr. Brooks how can we help you? My name is Guy Thomas we meet briefly before."

"Yea you came to my house" Karlon says. "Your just who I want to talk to. You were looking for information on the website and I have decided to answer any questions you may have regarding it"

"Well." Mr. Thomas says "let's go inside to my office sit down and talk. Would you like some coffee or something?"

Karlon replies "no thanks I'm good."

Mr. Thomas says, "Ok then my first question is where did this website come from? What was its purpose at Inception?"

Karlon answers," the purpose of the website was to allow black business owners to communicate with each other products and services they are selling or providing. Many black business owners complain that they were not getting support from the black community or other black businesses so this website allows them to shop for products and services sold and provided by black business owners."

Mr. Thomas then ask," is there a fee for this website use or membership?" Karlon replies, "No, there is no fee. However there are some minor rules and regulations that members must follow regarding the website."

Mr. Thomas then ask," How many members do you currently have? "Karlon replies, "At the moment the membership is 1988."

Mr. Thomas says, "So I know that I referred to it as a black business website, but do you have a name for your website group or organization?" Karlon replies, "No at this time I have or we have not given it a name, it's just a group of people communicating with each other on a website." Mr. Thomas is this the only thing that is going on within the website? Karlon replies," No actually we are beginning to use these communication for other things that may benefit each local community. Owners are branching out their services and volunteering to help in other ways other than their businesses. Some owners have dual occupations such as lawyers that own construction companies or as doctors that own corner stores. These are benefits that we can use to help their community in different ways." Mr. Thomas asked "okay Mr. Brooks where do you fit in in this organization what is your title or position?" Well Karlon replies," It looks like I've been strapped as the owner being that I was the one that started it. With it comes the responsibility of increasing the membership holding the members to the rules and regulations that we have agreed upon. I want to say that there is no money involved in the website no financial transactions are done on the website there is no salary involved in my position. Once the owner's contact each other on the website as far as what services and products they would like to buy from this particular business they call them directly and do business that way." Mr. Thomas ask, "How has this or has it affected your personal life, are there any drawbacks?" Karlon answers, "Actually I'm going to answer no to that question Mr. Thomas. I do consider myself a little busier with the fact that I still have a job managing Delicatessen & Catering operations and the fact that I'm expecting a child soon by my fiancé."

Well Mr. Brooks Thomas says," being that your website has no name how do you expect to advertise for it?"

Karlon says, "That's a good question." Karlon replies, "we have put it to the members for suggestions, but as for now it's just by word of mouth of the owners and their communities spreading the word that way. I will consider that giving the website a name because you have made a good suggestion."!

Karlon thinks about the point that Mr. Thomas made all the way home. Yeah I think we do need a name Karlon thinks to himself, he's right about the advertising and need to put this to the members and get some suggestions as far as a name and going forward is concerned.

Karlon gets to work the next day and the first thing he says to Bill, "Yes I think it's time for us to put a name on the website.

Bill replies, "yeah I agree."

Karlon replies, "So I'm going to put it to the members and see what they come up with. Karlon then post a message on the website to the members. After speaking with a member of the media and updating him on information concerning the website a suggestion was put to me as far as getting a name for our organization and website so at this time I do agree it's time to do so and we'll put it to the members as for a name for our organization, so please post any suggestions for names on the website and we will select the most popular and appropriate name

In a message posted on the website two weeks later. Karlon writes "I want to thank our members for their cooperation, patience and suggestions. At this time I would like to announce the name that our organization shall be recognized as is, THE NEW COMMUNITY this is what has been chosen. Please adhere to the rules and regulations that are already in place, under this name I believe we will expand and benefit our local communities with ease. However I do see broad changes being made to do so. maybe not immediately but in the near future. For as our membership grows I believe we will need to make possible positions that can handle certain matters. Requests have been made for our assistance that at this time is beyond our means but also donations to our organization have been offered that we are not able to take, but these are both matters that are at top priority. Having said that we are preparing to show our first public support for our member Lamont Lee in Jacksonville, NC. at his political rally and speech. We are asking local members to stand together and show support as The New Community. I understand that tee- shirts and signs have been made. I will monitor the election and give a report on the website, in closing I will announce our new membership total is 3,532. Thank you all for the support and cooperation."

Back at work Karlon seeks advice from Bill in reference to positions in the organization. Karlon asked Bill," What do you think about the positions I need to fill."

Bill replies, "you have 3,000 members to give you ideas,do as you did before putting it to.your membership. "Bill replies what do you need?

Karlon replies,"+ if we're going to be taking in donations or contributions we're going to need a treasure to keep a record of all money going in and out." Bill quickly raised his hand with a smile on his face,He says" me me me please, I'll hold all the money."

Karlon replies, "not a chance, I don't want to see you in a new silk suit each week. And do we need to incorporate or something? I need someone under me to be in charge if I'm not available, or someone on the west coast, someone in the north and south for local branches,I can't be travelling like that if someone is needed in person. I will go through the directory to get some ideas on people I can trust and I will decide on who will take what positions I'm not going to put it to a vote. But for right now I'm going to check on the election down south in Jacksonville and see what's going on." Karlon places a call to Mr. Lee, "Hey! Lamont talk to me how did you do?"

Mr. Lee replies, "You don't know? I won big time, man you should have seen the turnout. It seems signs and tee shirts with NEW COMMUNITY made us popular. People are coming in asking to join the organization, and what can they do."

Karlon replies, "I'm sure your speeches to had something to do with it too. Your platform of doing the right thing for the people, and a better future for them was very attractive.

"Well" Mr. Lee says" thanks for the support of THE NEW COMMUNITY and beware I am always at your disposal"

Karlon, "Good luck Lamont I will pass on the news to the membership."

A week later Karlon post on the website.

Dear members I would like to update you on current events involving the New Community. First and foremost I would like to congratulate Mr. Lamont Lee on being elected to councilman in Jacksonville, N.C. And he thanks the New Community for support that he feels had a lot to do with his success. As I said before the new community is evolving to do bigger and better things in the community local and Nationwide. I am now appointing people in positions that will allow us to do bigger and better things. We will be allowing local cities to build their own website which will allow them to do things in their community that best suits them. We will begin to allow new members that are not business owners to join in order for them to lend a hand in their Community to make it better. However they will be doing their business on a separate website.

After posting on the website Karlon decides to have a heart-to-heart conversation with Bill

.Karlon says, "Who do you think knows most about the website and what we are doing other than me? Do you think can handle this type of business on the scale that we are doing it other than me? I need someone to be in charge if I am not around to answer questions or make decisions."

Bill responded, "Why are you looking at me funny, I think you are talking about me. Man you're smart, yep you are the answer. But not going to push you in, think on it and answer what's best for you." "Man you should be a salesman," Karlon says. By the way call Randy he asked to speak to you.

Bill calls immediately." Hey Randy what's up, Karlon said you looking for me." Randy replies, "yes I wanted to ask you about them police and the trash cans. Did you get a lawyer on it? Bill, replies, "Yes, we are about to meet with the police it seems as if maybe they wanted to cut a deal rather than go to court and fight because the lawyer told them we have video.

"Okay" Randy replies, "Do you need me, I will be available if you do just call me, I will not let them get away with that. As a matter of fact maybe there's some things he can do for the New Community."

Bill say "Yea Mr. O. Simmons he is pretty sharp. He was at the meeting, and he is down for helping out. I will talk to Karlon and suggest that to him."

Karlon places s call to Mr. Simmons. "Hello Mr. Simmons, Karlon Brooks here calling to ask a few questions about organizing The New Community. We are being offered donations that we are not organized enough to take. Well actually I'm asking if you would be available to be the lawyer for The New Community."

Mr. Simmons responds, "I would be honored, but at this time I feel it would be too much for my plate. But would you be open to me having a partner in order to handle the workload of my private business and The Business of the new community?" Karlon replies, "That's fine with me, I think that's even better.

Simmons replied, "I do have someone in mind already, Mr. Jim Davis,not actually my partner at this time but I know he is a good man and would be willing to help out in any way he can.

Davis & Simmons sounds like a good name"

Karlon, ". What we need to do is get everything legal so that our organization is on the books properly and donations and such can be accounted for. Okay Mr. O, do what you need to do to organize and I will back you up just keep me updated as to what's going on,"

A couple of days later

Karlon calls Randy ", It looks as if we are going to court about the garbage tickets the lawyer wants the police department to be exposed for this offense and I agree with him. So we may be calling on you and Bill to testify at some point or another.

Randy replies, "yeah man I think that's a good thing to do rather than settling out of court because if we do that no one will know what they done it's more the principle of the matter than anything else so I'm down just give me a call."

And just like that 3 weeks later the court date arrives. Ali, Jerome, Randy, Karlon, and Bill are present. Ms. Simmons puts Jerome on the stand first. Please explain the events when you arrived to the store the morning in question.

Jerome answers, "Well sir as I arrived to the store I noticed a summons stuck to the door. I did read that it was regarding the trash in the back. After reading it I continued opening the store, and after I entered I went to the back to observe the trash. I did notice that there was trash on the ground, and two of the trash cans were also tipped over. So I continued my job while waiting for Bill to arrive"

Mr. Simmons next question, "Jerome can you tell if the sanitation dept. had collected the trash?"

Jerome replies, "yes and no, I could tell that they had not picked up the trash as of yet."

Mr. Simmons asked again, "can you tell me what you did next Jerome?"

Jerome replies, "Yes I picked up the trash and put all the trash that was on the ground into the can and I put the top back on to the trash can."

Mr. Simmons asked," "Okay" Jerome this is my final question. Did the sanitation department eventually pick up the trash that was left and the can?"

Jerome replied, "Yes they did come and pick up the cans and trash later on"

. Mr. Simmons says, "Okay Jerome that's all the questions I have for you right now thank you very much"

. Mr. Simmons address Court right now I'd like to call Mr. Ali Martin to the stand.

Mr Simmons asked Ali, can you please tell us what was the status of the garbage cans the night before you left the store. Ali replies "I left four cans full of garbage with four tops locked on top of them. There was no garbage on the ground.

Mr. Simmons asked. Can you tell us is that the normal amount of garbage?"

Then Ali replies, "No sir there is usually two cans of garbage but there was a meeting in the dining hall and that left four cans full."

Mr. Simmons responded "Thank you sir that's all the questions I have for you." Now your honor"

Mr. Simon says, "I would like to produce video evidence of the next sequence, after Ali left the store and Jerome came in the next morning Mr. Simmons approach the video camera and started it. It shows patrol car number 412 Patrolling in front of the store. As the car passes by the cans the passenger door opens and rubs up against all the cans but only two cans fall and garbage is left on the ground. Half an hour later it shows the same car number 412 coming in front of the store and an officer gets out and places a summons on the door of the store.

Mr. Simmons now ask the judge "I would like to call officer Mullen to the stand." After officer Mullen was sworn in Mr. Simmons asked him "are you the officer driving car number for 12 on the night in question?"

The officer replied, "Yes I was driving that car that night." Mr. Simmons asked "Can you tell us the name of your partner in the passenger seat on that night?"

The officer replies, "My partner was officer Blattner."

Mr. Simmons asked did you see officer Blattner open the passenger door as he passed in front of the garbage cans I'm front of the store. "The officer replied, "yes I did, but I don't know why it was done."

Simmons says, "Thank you officer Mullen that's all I have for you today. I would now like to call officer Blattner to the stand". Officer Blattner comes to stand and is sworn in. This question is asked officer Blattner for the night in question, "can you tell us why you open the car door in front of the garbage cans?"

Officer Blattner replied," I opened the door in order to expectorate."

Okay Mr. Simmons replied," can you tell us then why you gave a summons to the store when you know you were the one that knocked over the cans?"

Officer Blattner replied, "I did what I was ordered to do". Mr. Simmons asked, "On the previous night officer, you came to this address and came inside to ask questions correct?"

"Yes" the officer replied, "Simmons, Were you under orders to do so?"

"No" the officer replied,

Mr. Simmons then. Asked, "So can you tell us why you did this?" Officer replied, "I saw a lot of cars in the parking lot and I took it upon myself to see what was going on inside".

Well, sir replied Mr. Simmons, "you saw a lot of cars in the parking lot. Was there any illegal activities that you saw in the parking lot?"

"Well actually no" replied the officer

Mr. Simmons, "So what was it that was suspicious that made you go inside?"

The officer replies "Instincts is the only answer I can give you". The officer replied.

Simmons, "Once you went inside officer you asked questions about the meeting inside the catering hall, Correct?"

The officer replied "Yes."

Simmons, "When asked about your presence there and you replied that you are under orders, correct?"

"Yes" replied the officer

Simmons, "But officer was this actually true? You were not under orders to go inside this establishment, were you?"

Actually no. the officer replied.

Simmons, "So officer just to review the evening you see cars in the parking lot that you felt were suspicious so your instinct tells you to go inside and find out what was going on once you got inside you asked questions and told them you are under orders to do so. After leaving, later on in the morning you come around knocked their garbage cans over and then give them a ticket for unsanitary garbage. And you replied earlier that you were given orders to give them a summons. Was this true?"

"No" the officer replied.

Simmons, "Okay Officer you can step down. That's all I have for you today." After this the lawyer for the city asked the judge, "Can we meet in chambers your honor?"

And he replies, "Yes, I think that is best." After arriving in chambers the lawyer for the city says "Your honor I see no reason to continue, the city would like to concede at this point"

The judge responded by saying, "If by doing this you think your officer is going to get away with lying on the stand you are sadly mistaken. And I know you wish to avoid any further embarrassment. Your officer is going to be charged with a misdemeanor count of perjury."

Mr. Simmons says, "Also I believe that we should consider civil rights violations against my client by the city."

The judge says, "Ok look I'm going to deliberate for about 30 minutes, and I will give you my decision." After 30 minutes the judge returns and says, "I have no reason and have not been given any justified reason why this was done. I am awarding Mr. Graves $15,000 for his time and damages in addition civil rights violations by the officer which the city is responsible for. And in addition to paying his legal fees. This is my decision court is adjourned."

Randy, Bill, Jerome, Ali and Karlon all leave the courtroom. They all meet in the parking lot and

Randy says "15 grand how we gonna split that up?"

Jerome says, "Let's get some steak and lobster that's my idea."

Bill replies, "We ain't doing that. I'll figure out something better to do with the money. I'll see you guys back at the store." But before Karlon goes to the store he decides to check on Samira who is staying at her mom's house during her late months of pregnancy. But just as he pulls in front of the house her older brother is bringing her out to the car.

"Hey! What's up? Karlon yells.

"My water broke." Samira replies.

"Ok get in my car Karlon says". In what seemed like 3.5 seconds they arrive at the hospital. They get to the emergency room and Announced her water broke. A nurse comes to take Samira in for preparation.

She asked Karlon, "Are you going in for the delivery?"

Karlon says, "as much as I would like the answer is no, I would most definitely faint if I was in there." So Karlon stays in the waiting room with her brother Joe and Sister Barbara. It took about 4 hours but the nurse comes out and yells Karlon Brooks, Karlon gets up and the nurse dresses him to go in the room as he gets closer to the baby she says, "it's a boy congratulations".

Karlon gets to go in to see Samira and she opens her eyes and says, "Thanks for the beautiful baby boy"

Karlon says, "Your welcome but it's me that should be thanking you."

"I love you baby." he says as he leaves out.

Karlon returns to the waiting room and announces that "Karlon Brooks Junior is in the building". As he says this Joe and Barbara come to the window for the nurse to display the baby. Karlon heads back to the store, but on his way he stops to buy some cigars that say "It's a boy" on them. Karlon is so hyped up he passes out cigars to some strangers. But arrives back at the store to announce to his fellow coworkers and Bill.

Bill asked, "Do you need the rest of the day off?"

Karlon says, "No"

Bill yells, "Ok! Then let's get some work done."

Karlon says, "Actually Bill it's all good, in-store supplies are good, no events on schedule. But I do need to tend to New Community stuff." Karlon sees message from Jim Davis so he gives him a call.

Karlon, "Hey Mr. Davis I see that you called me I wanted to give you a call back I did not hear your message but what do you have going on that I need to hear about."

Davis says, "Brooks I'm glad you called that I have some news for you about the organization. We do have a bank account under the name of the community and we are holding on to some checks that are for donations. At this time these checks need to be signed by you before deposit. I do wish to tell you that these checks are coming in continually so people are donating at a good rate

Karlon replies, "All that sounds good. But I would like for you to keep a separate tab on donations and amounts that are given by each person."

"No problem" Jim replies, "The question is what's next"

Karlon says, "Well what I would like to do is get some big name donations behind us to put us in a larger light."

Jim say, "I think I can help with that, but don't want to make no promises too soon, I will let you know. The vision break out to the public."

After a couple of days Mr. Davis calls back to Karlon to give him some names.

Davis says, "How would you like to speak to a movie producer. Mr. Lee and professional athlete Mr. Pierce."

Karlon replies, "That seem like a meeting I need a suit and tie for. Will I meet both of them at the same time?"

Davis responds, "No that's not the plan I just wanted to let you know I had someone speak to them separately about you and they are interested in meeting you and talking to you about the new community, and the direction you plan to go with it."

Karlon says, "Okay that's fine just set up time and date and I will make myself available for each one."

Davis, "Okay but let me give you one tip about talking to them. Do not mention money or any amount, let them do that. Just tell them your plans and at the end, ask for suggestions and what they think about your plans and what you want to do."

Karlon, "Okay that sounds like good advice thanks for the hookup I'll let you know how it works out after I have met with both of them"

Davis, "And by the way I understand you are a new father so congratulations on that."

Karlon replies, "thank you sir."

Two days later Karlon gets a call. "Hello Mr. Brooks."

"Yes hello" Karlon replies,

"Yes sir this is Mr. Lee I understand there is a meeting we need to have."

"Yes sir" Karlon says, "hoping you have an opening in your schedule."

"No problem brother" Lee says, "I'm open. I got nothing going on so I'll leave it to you."

Karlon, "If you do that give me an address I will be there tomorrow high noon."

Lee laughs" ok see you then."

Next day at 5 minutes before 12 noon Karlon gets off the elevator headed towards Mr. Lee's office. After the receptionist makes Karlon comfortable in a waiting chair Mister Lee presents himself. "Karlon Brooks glad to see you brother come on In" Mr. Lee says. Mr. Lee continues before we get started I would like to present to you one rule I have with these meetings, and that is that they ought to be informal at the rawest form. I even allow cursing. I want you to be relaxed in order to express to me your true thoughts and feelings about what you want to say. So if that's okay with you I will call you Karlon you can call me Lee. So bro tell me how we got here, what's the delay with your new community. Tell me how it started and where you want to go with it."

Karlon replies, "To tell you the truth man if I look back at it, it all seems like a blur at times. I remember having a conversation with my boss slash friend slash Mentor Bill G about the difficulty of black businesses and black business men, I actually tried to start my own business at one point but was shot down with the credit bureau boys. So me and Billy got into a conversation about black businesses and the difficulty they have in the community. Most black business owners complain that black money is not kept in the black community. We also talked about black business is doing business with other black businesses to keep black money in the community. And it came up that one of the reasons black businesses have problems is that black business owners don't know what products and services other black owners may be supplying. So I came up with the idea of a website where all black businesses can register and state what products and services they Supply so other black businesses and the public can deal with them directly. It seems to have grown to the point where we needed administer rules and to pick officers in the group to manage certain aspects of the website. Whereas we had this meeting and it drew some people from Faraway places and gave me an idea of how far the website has reached. As a matter of fact we reached out in North Carolina to help one of our members get elected to a political office there.

Lee says, "Yo! That's what's up. You got it like that?"

Karlon replies with a laugh and says, "I can't actually say that, but now it seems that the new community has reached into the political arena a bit. So now I'm feeling that there may be more that we can do and I want there to be no limit as to how far we can go in the community and nationally helping our people. I have sought some legal advice and have tried to put the new community in a legal position to accept donations. I have also a meeting coming up with a pro athlete Mr Pierce.

"Hold up" Lee says, "Really, if you want I can do that for you. I talk to him often. He is definitely down for the cause. And as for what I'm hearing from you I am too. You are coming from a unique perspective, what you are trying to do?"

Karlon," I would like for are communication level to reach out to more black businesses so the benefit of the website can reach far and wide. I would like to meet with Mr. Pierce myself but have no problem with you talking to him."

Lee," Ok let's meet him together." Lee suggest

"Now that's cool." Karlon says.

Lee, "Ok. Karlon look, I'm not going to hand you a million dollar check today, so let's get together with Mr. Pierce and see where it leads us."

Back at home and back to work Karlon has a conversation with Bill G. (Sounding a little upset)

Bill Says, "I'm starting to have a problem with your schedule my son"

Karlon says, "Yeah, I can understand that but at the same time my responsibilities are being done I'm just not here in the present.

Bill replies, "Yeah that's one of my points, you seem to be making your own schedule."

Karlon replies, "(in an argumentative tone) you know what I'm doing and what I'm faced with. It's not like I'm out running the streets or in the movie theater or something."

Bill replies, "as much as I understand the importance of what you're doing it's getting to the point where you may need to make a choice.

Karlon replies, "Well again I understand your argument I think it's just that I need to handle more things concerning the new community during my off hours.

Bill, "Yea that's my point."

Karlon, "Ok look all of my information on the new community is on my computer at home also I just need an office space. So if it's okay with you I will come to the store on my off-hours and use a computer here that will give me more space to do what I need.

Bill responds, "That's fine, I have no problem with that but I need you here when you're supposed to be here period."

Karlon, "Now I do have one big meeting to handle with a Mr. Lee and Mr. Pierce so I may need to schedule that meeting at their convenience so I need to get back to you on that. Or actually has it just came to my mind, maybe I can use the catering hall for the meeting with them. But I may need to do so Incognito because I don't know if these guys want the attention if they are recognized. Mr. Lee produces movies and Mr. Pierce is a pro athlete." Karlon makes a call to Mr. Lee.

Karlon, "Hey look I may have a scheduling problem for our meeting with Mr. Pierce. Is it possible for you guys to come to East Orange New Jersey where I manage a delicatessen with Bill G. the guy I mentioned to you? We can use our catering hall for the meeting. I don't know if you guys want to go incognito and use the side entrance of the catering hall."

Lee replies, "No that's not actually necessary I am not and I don't believe that my buddy is not afraid of our public"

". So how about this" Karlon says, "you guys can come in the side door of the catering hall we can have our meeting and then you guys can present yourselves to the customers and maybe sign a couple of autographs which you know is going to be requested."

"Okay" Lee replies, "I think that will be fun, it's not a problem, trust me."

Karlon, "Thanks bro I'll see you then." Karlon then has a conversation with Bill G.

Karlon says, "Look. I am going to use the catering hall for the meeting with Mr. Lee and Pierce and they may come out and sign some autographs with the customers so that might be good for business also.

Bill reply, "yeah that's cool."

Karlon says to him, "but also do not advertise this because I don't have an exact date for a meeting and I don't want people to know ahead of time that they are coming that may cause chaos and we don't want that."

"Ok no chaos" Bill replied. "But let's clean up good as to give a good impression. Have someone stock supply shelfs. On day of meeting have all partial meats pulled out." Yes sir" Karlon replied, "So for now I will get a date and let you know."

Two days later

Karlon tells "Bill they are coming tomorrow at 1 p.m."

Bill replies, "Have a tray of food made for them in case they are hungry and in order to advertise what we have in case we can get some clients from them."

Karlon replies "I've already done that, the menu for the platter is on my desk." Next day arrives Karlon is waiting by the side entrance of the dining hall when he sees a black limo pull up, so no doubt this is them it opens the door the limo stops and outcomes Lee and Pierce.

Karlon," Welcome gentlemen hope you had a pleasant ride come on inside and make yourself comfortable. But before you sit down I would like you to see an assortment of foods in case you guys are hungry and I would like for you to see what we can offer as far as catering in case you guys know of any clients that would like to have us serve their functions. But for now I would like to bring in Mr. Bill G who is the owner of this establishment, so take a look at the platter I'll be right back." Karlon and Bill come back into the hall.

Karlon "hello gentlemen this is Mr. Bill G. Bill this is Mr. Lee and Mr. Pierce.

Lee says, "Nice catering hall you have here Bill, how many people does it hold?

Bill, "replies the actual number is 250 that we serve here comfortably."

Lee, "okay Mr. Bill that's good to know."

Bill replies, Hey you know what you guys I'm going to step out this meeting is between you guys Karlon is the one that is calling the shots as far as the new community is concerned, if you need anything from me and the establishment I'm right here to serve.

Lee, "Okay so let's get down to business Mr. Brooks I would like for you to tell Mr. Pierce in your own words why we are here I did give him a brief summary but it comes better from you with the heart."

"yes Mr. Brooks" Mr. Pierce says," I have heard good things but maybe there are some things Lee told me that you would like to add to. I am pretty sure Lee told you his rule of informal meetings so that still applies so hit me up with what you got." Karlon replies, "Well look it all started because I got frustrated that I did not get an opportunity to start my own business because of my credit issues. Me and Bill got into a discussion of how difficult it is for blacks to start and maintain businesses in the black community. I came up with one idea that most black businesses have problems in the community because other black businesses don't know what products and services they are selling or providing. So I came up with the idea of starting a website where black business owners can post their businesses and the name and products they are selling or providing and leaving contact information for other owners to contact them for business purposes. We did get a flux of members to join and got a flow of businesses to start communications to the point where we had a meeting of the owners to do more organizing. In the process of that we got one of our members elected to a public office because of the growth of the membership in that area. I am now wondering just how far this can go and how much we can do for blacks and the black community nationwide. I am set up legally for the new community to be able to receive donations but I wish to broaden our ability to do more. So this is where we are. Lee asks, "Let me ask you a question? What is it that we can do to help you?"

Karlon replies (with a laugh), "You can pass off that million dollar check you mentioned last week." (They all laughed for a minute)

Karlon says, "I know you guys know a lot of people in your separate professions and basically I need help doing just what I'm trying to do. And that is, spread the word to as many business or should I say black business owners as possible. And actually I would like to access some of those big connections you have sports stars and movie stars and such your connections reach across the country just as I'm trying to do. This will help as many communities as we can reach Nationwide.

Mr. Pierce then asked, "what is the endgame what is it that you hope to accomplish if you consider yourself on this journey to be successful?"

Karlon then replies. "Well I first of all I feel that we as blacks don't get a fair Shake in doing things that we want to do such as businesses and loans and housing. I feel one way for us to get a fair chance is if we are judged by our people in our community. For black businesses to be able to strengthen themselves by doing business with each other and help their individual communities. For black businesses to grow stronger in the community where they can help the people of the community in more ways by helping people with loans. Black real estate helping people get better housing to help keep the black money in the black communities for black businesses to be as free from white help as possible and be independent from that. For far too long we have been under the thumb of an oppressor

Pierce says, "Man you got a head on you how old are you?"

.Karlon replies I'm 22.

Pierce, "And by the way congratulations Mr. Brooks I understand you are a new father Pierce says."

Karlon, "Thanks bro. Karlon L Brooks Jr. Is in the game now. Born nov.30th".

Lee says, "how you doing with that bro?"

Karlon, "It's my first one. Best thing I can do is the best I can do."

Pierce, "never heard that approach before but it sounds good. Hey look I've heard enough, if I hear too much more my head will explode. So enough of the meeting me and Lee will talk. Let us take a look at the rest of the store. I'm pretty sure you have customers that would like to get some autographs once they see my pretty face.

So Karlon takes Lee and Pierce out into the store to the kitchen so they can see the place where food is prepared for catering jobs. But as they were passing through the deli store someone noticed." Oh crap" someone said, "That's Mr. Lee." As we walk into the kitchen.

Pierce says, "Wow this is a big kitchen and I see you have walk-in refrigerators and a big freezer you must do some serious cooking in here."

Lee says, "I tell you what we can do from now on, if we need to have any meetings with other people concerning the new community you can have them here in your catering hall. This will also allow other people to see what you can do. Okay let's go back out into the store I heard someone yelling already, let's sit down for a bit.

Karlon, "I hope you're up to signing some autographs." Lee and Pierce walk out into the deli, people started clapping and yelling. Another guy walks up closer and says alright you're Antonio Pierce,

He asks, "Can I get a pic real quick?"

"That's cool" Pierce says, "hook it up. What's your name bro? Maybe I want a copy of the picture too."

The guy laughs "my name is Quincey, most people call me Q, and I know you don't want no picture of me in your wallet." After a couple of minutes it starts to get a little more crowded at the store as people notice what's going on inside. So Lee and Pierce continue to sign autographs talk to the customers and take pictures but Lee, "says it may be time to pull out."

Pierce says, "So let's hit it".

Lee says to Karlon, "We're going to pull out and me and Pierce will talk and we will get back to you on any ideas that we have for your new community but meanwhile keep doing what you're doing, I am very impressed."

Karlon says, "Hey guys thanks for coming it was nice to meet you, MR. Pierce hope to hear from you soon".

Karlon goes back to Bills office,

Karlon asked "hey what do you think?"

Bill replies, "Well they seem to be impressed and interested in what you are saying and what you are doing. I believe they got a good look at the store and hopefully they will send us some business of a high caliber." And as they talk the phone rings and Karlon pic's up.

"Hey, Karlon it's Kelvin. How are you? I'm calling to let you know there's a guy interested in having us get together as a group and having us sing a song that he wrote and maybe record it. What do you think? Are you interested?"

Karlon replies, "Yeah I'm interested have you talked to Herb and Victor already? Yeah I asked both of them already and they are down with it so it's up to you. So I will call him let him know we will do it and let's get a date to meet him hear the song and practice it. Ok that's is cool. Holla back with the info.

Bill Interjects, "Karlon I heard your conversation I'm pretty sure you have enough on your plate already what are you doing?" Karlon responds, "Hey look I can do some things in my spare time, that don't take a lot of energy to do plus it's something that we all have wanted to do for a long time, even though it did not come to us while we were singing on a regular basis. Look I'm on my way home now and Samira is complaining that the baby is not well so I'm going to check on them now I'll talk to you later. Karlon gets home. Samira address him as soon as he gets in and says, "It does not seem to be getting any better we may need to consider taking him to the doctor in the morning or emergency room tonight."

"Okay" Karlon replies, "what is his temperature have you been checking it and has it changed at all recently."

"That's my point" she replies, "nothing has changed and he does not seem comfortable and is breathing seems difficult." Karlon, "Ok I will monitor him for a while just to see what's going on, I know I'm not a doctor but I will get a better feel for what's going on myself." In the morning. Karlon wakes up and checks on the status of the baby. He then calls Samira and says to her "okay let's get things together and take the baby to the doctor." As they are getting dressed Karlon gets a phone call from Kelvin and

Kelvin says," okay bro are you available tonight we can go and rehearse with this time and see what's going on."

Karlon replies, "Things are a little sketchy here with the baby being sick so promises are hard to come by so I will take it by ear and see how the baby is doing. I do not want to leave her with the baby because it will not seem right. I will get back to you." After arriving at the doctor's office. The doctor examines Karlon Junior and says to the parents I think you need to get the baby to the hospital he has pneumonia and needs to be treated soon.

Karlon answers, "Okay we are on our way right now." As they get to the hospital and sign up on the incoming sheet

The nurse says, "Your doctor called and you can bring the baby right now we have a room for him." As they get to the room being prepared for the baby Karlon and Samira are asked to step outside the room while they get the baby in bed.

Karlon asked after seeing what was being prepared for the baby "What is all this stuff why does the bed need to be covered?"

The nurse responds, "this is what they do Mr Brooks for the babies protection." Karlon and Samira sit alongside the baby's bed just looking. Karlon just happened to look up and who is standing there but

Kelvin "What's up man how is the baby? What's wrong?"

Karlon says, "They said pneumonia."

"Can we go or what" Kelvin asked. Just as he said that Samira lifts up her head, and gave Kelvin an answer.

Karlon, "Look man you know that's not a priority right now. Let me talk to Samira alone for a minute." So Kelvin steps out.

Karlon says, "Look, I don't want to leave and I know you don't want me to leave so I'm going to tell him to practice without me. I don't want you shooting fireballs at me with your eyes all night." Samira says, "No you can go I will stay here."

Karlon, "how about this I will go only if they come to Newark to practice instead of going out to Plainfield. So they can push practice back a day or two and maybe the baby will be better by then. And when I go I will come right back here and you can leave and go home and get some rest and I will stay. So the deal is set and done." Karlon and the group have their rehearsal and when Karlon gets back Samira is sleep. Karlon nudges her to let her know she can go home. But she says to him, "I'm staying because the doctor say we may all be able to go home today." So Karlon and Samira wait for doctor's word, and it is good. Karlon Jr. can go home with doctor's instructions and medications for Karlon Jr. after returning home and settling in Karlon discusses the need for cell phones. After agreeing Karlon set straight out to buy cell phones for the parents before returning to work. Karlon head straight to Bill to inform him of the new cell phone numbers.

Bill says, "That's a good idea for you as new parents and maybe it will help our communication to."

Karlon says, "Okay right now I'm going to get things ready for catering the meeting for the women's group tomorrow. All supplies are in. All the servers have been informed of their reporting times and responsibilities. I just need three people to start setting up the catering hall for the function, who do we have available?"

Bill says, "Take Linda Debbie and Steve." Karlon goes out into the Delicatessen to grab his three people to help him

. Karlon says, "Okay Good we need to set up today for the women's meeting tomorrow all the decorations are on the front table and the chairs need to be set up. Ok we got it, it should only take us about an hour and a half. I'll be here for a while if you need me. Karlon heads back to office as he hears phone ringing. Hello Karlon it's Mr. Lee what's good bro

Karlon replies, "Hey man I was just stepping into office as phone rang, what's good with you? You busy man? I can call back." Lee says, "No dude better now than later, what's up?" Karlon replied. "Got some more peeps that maybe interested but you may need to reel them in. in addition to that I may have some ideas for you, that you may want to consider. What I'm considering is in conference call to have some people that are at a distance to hear your ideas."

"Ok." Karlon replies, "When do we do this? How 'bout tomorrow at 1pm I got others in different time zone" Lee says. "That's good for me" Karlon says.

Next day 1pm Karlon finishes update to members on website. The phone rings Karlon picks up and answers, "hello this is Karlon"

"Hey Karlon this is Lee hold on for a minute you will hear a couple of clicks as I add all the people to this conference call." Lee comes back on," Okay Karlon let me tell you who is on the line first there is Michael Bennett from the NFL, also we have Mr. Charles Dutton who needs no introduction, we also have a real estate Agent

Mr James Douglas. And finally we have another private investor. Mr. Joe Cotton. Gentleman the next voice you hear will be Karlon Brooks.

"Hello gentlemen, I first would like to thank you for your time and interest in the new community. Which came about do to my realization as to how hard it is for African Americans to open businesses or get business loans. I've heard plenty of times that black businesses don't get support from the black community, so I devised a way for the community and black businesses to communicate with each other by offering a website where black businesses can list what services or products they sell. In the process of doing this I have learned number one, how many people are interested in this. I see the increase of memberships grow rapidly. I also have found that this forum can be used in other ways to help the black community and it has come to light in the way of helping one of our members be elected to a city post. And so I am open to any ideas that you guys may have in order to help the success of this organization in helping our people be better people to one another. We can do better if we are judged by one another, rather than by white people. We have a better chance at being judged fairly. "So Karlon went on with his presentation opening eyes and quietly impressing the group. After he finished,

Karlon asked, "if there were any questions from any of the listeners."

"Hello" a voice said this is Charles Dutton I understand that you manage a delicatessen in East Orange New Jersey. How do you find time to do this and your job? And by the way I also understand you are a new father so congratulations on that. Karlon replies, "Yes, Mr. Dutton right now I am merging my time between new community and my responsibilities at work on the same computer. Mr. Dutton replies," you are aware that if the new community is to evolve then your time spent on it needs to increase.

Yes sir, Karlon says, I understand that. Up to this point I have been pretty flexible, your point is valid so it is something I need to increase".

At that time another voice says, "May I address the elephant in the room?." This is Joe Cotton. What are you looking for financially?"

Well Sir Karlon replies, "I am not in a position to ask for a specific amount, at this point I tried to accumulate as many donations as I can and take my actions according to how much funding is available to me"

. Mr. Cotton then ask, "Are you willing to share the funding responsibilities and actions with others?"

Karlon replies," yes sir I am."

"Okay Karlon" Lee says, "As usual we will get together as a group and discuss where we are financially and get back to you at the next meeting. But I hope you are willing to travel because I am thinking about bringing you out to Los Angeles to meet these people in person and I have a couple of other ideas I think will bring in more donations.

"That's fine Mr. Lee, "Karlon says," I look forward to our next meeting and wish to thank you all for your time and efforts and listening to what I have in mind for the new community."

7 board and bank

After speaking with the proposed donors on the phone, Karlon retreats to his office in the store to meditate. Just as the quietness seems to be comfortable Bill comes in to break the silence.

Bill, "I guess you're meditating on what changes need to be made around here regarding your schedule Bill asked?"

Karlon replied, No I am just wondering how much these guys are going to donate to the new community and I have a feeling they want to make some changes as to how things are being done financially. I am willing to listen to ideas but I am going to keep things as they are, whereas the members as a whole are the ones that make the decisions. I'm not going to let them determine how things go because of the amount of money they donate. But as things stand right now I'm just going to wait and see rather than try to predict the future, so we'll see in a couple of days what they come back with."

After a couple of days Lee calls,

Lee, "hey Karlon can you come to the city Thursday?"

Karlon, "yes what up what you got going on?" Well I'm going to be on a show called Midday Live, you heard of it?"

"Yes" Karlon replied."

Lee, "I want to introduce you and your cause to the public."

Karlon "Ok do I need a tux?"

Lee laughed, "No but don't wear no jeans and sneakers either. Meet me at my office 10 a.m. and we will ride there and I will explain the do's and don'ts okay?"

Karlon, "Okay I got it Lee." But after he hung up the phone from talking with Mr. Lee Karlon pretty much burned out his fingers calling everybody telling them he was going to be on TV. Now Karlon gets home and has to answer some tough questions from Samira.

Samira, "So Mr. Lee invite you to be on TV can I come with you? I know I'm not going to be on TV but it would not be nice to come along?"

Karlon reply ``Yeah, I think that would be okay, I don't think Lee would mine but I'm going to ask him anyway just to make sure that it's okay for you to come." So Karlon put in a call to Lee.

Karlon, "Hey dude minor question my soon-to-be wife wants to know if it's okay if she tagged along for the ride she doesn't want to be on TV she just wants to come along with us to the show".

Lee, "Yea man that's cool, I'm not surprised, it's common for the wife to come along, especially for the first time. But I want you to know that I mean for the first time because I believe we will do this again on another show so be prepared for that."

Karlon, "Okay my brother thanks, Karlon reply I'll see you then, we will be on time" Karlon and Samira arrive on time and get with Lee in the limo.

Samira, "It's nice to meet you Mr. Lee, thank you"

Mr. Lee replies, "same thing here it's an honor to meet you in person."

Lee, "Okay Karlon this is what's going to happen, after I go on stage and meet with the people we will get into a conversation and I will bring up your cause and introduce you. All you have to do is come out on stage greet the people express how nice it is to be here and begin to present your cause and how it got started. After your finish leave a telephone number and website information for people to call to join or get information on the New Community."

"Okay Karlon replies, I got it I'm cool."

Lee says, "It's a nice touch with the shirt and jacket you didn't overdo it and you didn't come gangsta either." Samira and Karlon both laugh. But as they do they arrive at the studio. And just as planned. Karlon stepped on stage with no nervousness and presented himself and the new community well.

Karlon, "Ladies as gentlemen my name is Karlon Brooks, I want to share with you a vision I see. We have all been told that black people don't work together. I have not known the reason for this but I feel

I can help with the solution. My vision is for us to help each other to the point where we are sufficient enough to succeed. To donate to volunteer, to reach out our hands when our neighbor needs help, by volunteering your time and labor. By donating money to help out. By volunteering skills and knowledge that you have that can help our people. We have black billionaires sport Stars and movie stars that can donate money. We have lawyers and doctors that can donate or volunteer their knowledge and skills. If this is done not just in one community, but across the nation we can make a difference. This is what our ancestors did to succeed, they stuck together and volunteered whatever they had in order to succeed. Many people in the black community always saying that the money in the black community does not stay in the community. What I see is black business owners doing business outside the community because they know not that there are black business owners in the community that can supply their needs. So I have designed a website for black business owners to register and advertise their products and services so they can do business in the community. This is something that can unite and bring them closer together. By keeping the money in the community not only is business better but the patrons do better. I'm calling on my people to come together and do better, to help each other. Help the man next to you. And in the words of the Great Robin Harris, not just the man next to you but the man next to the man." And people applauded after hearing his cause to the point where he got a standing ovation. After coming off stage

Lee said to Karlon, "I think that went better than I planned it to go so yes we will do this again." Next time I get an opportunity, but I think we will have another meeting with the proposed investors. So I think you're going to need to open up time on your schedule because we will be busy for the next week or two together.

"Okay" Karlon replies, I will have a conversation with Bill G because I do have a job, I don't know for how long but as of right now I am still working for him." So Karlon's next objective is to have another conversation with Bill G. When they arrive home Karlon heads right to the store to do just that. Just as Karlon gets into store

Bill yells out, "can I have your autograph you look good on TV and things came across well. So what will be your next move with Mr. Lee and the gang?"

Karlon replies, "yeah that's what we need to talk about are you busy?" After they sit down in the office

Bill says to Karlon, Are we going to have a conversation that we've already had before about your availability and time dedicated to the store and your job?"

"Yeah" Karlon replies, "I was just told by Lee that things are going to get a little more busier being that we publicize things on TV."

Bill asks, "Okay so what are you doing? Are you quitting or resigning?"

Karlon replies, "No, that's not my intention but I want to wait and see what happens at the next meeting, I think it's going to be what tells me what we need to do from here on out.

Bill ask, "When is this meeting supposed to take place?

Karlon says, "I'm waiting on a phone call and I'll let you know what the deal is because maybe this meeting may be here or in New York or on a conference call I will let you know either way. But before that I need to let you in on a little personal news. I have been thinking to ask Samira to marry me and if she says yes. At some point in time you will be catering the most important wedding reception the store has ever done."

Bill replies, "Wow let me know as soon as possible what your plans are as far as dates for your wedding and reception". After talking with Bill Karlon goes to the website to update all members, public, and business about the meeting with Mr. Lee and upcoming meeting with prospective donors.

Two days later Karlon gets a call from

Lee, "hello Karlon, 1 I'm calling to talk to you about the upcoming meeting are you busy can you talk now?"

Karlon reply "yeah what's up Lee you have my ear."

Lee, "+Okay listen I have two things, number one the meeting is going to take place one week from tomorrow at your place if it's available and there will be 20 people not including me and you. I know normally you will put out some food as a courtesy but, this meeting will be catered hopefully by you and Bill. The members that are coming are asking to pay for this catering in order to get a true sense of the service provided by the catering operation. I will give you the details on the menu and you can give me a price hopefully within 2 days from now. The other thing is there is another catering offer coming from another person that will be a higher clientele and larger volume affair I will send you the person's name and number for you to contact them and you and Bill can arrange the particulars on the affair. In the meeting that's coming at your hall we will discuss a more permanent operation for the new community and incoming donations and your position and involvement."

Karlon replies, "okay yes Lee we will be able to do the catering Affair here that will be no problem and I will offer a discount because it's new community business and I will also offer your contact a discount because it's coming from you."

Lee replies, "I don't think you have to worry about discounts with the people that you may be involved with because they are high clientele."

Karlon says, "That may be true but at the same time I think as a courtesy I will offer the discount. Also I would like to have the lawyers for new community there, is that okay? It's just two guys".

Lee, "We're not going to prosecute you Karlon."

Karlon, "Yeah I realize that Karlon says but I think it's a good idea on behalf of the new community to have them there maybe they can answer questions or even make suggestions according to what your people may propose or suggest." So Karlon goes to inform Bill about meeting and the prospective catering job.

Karlon, "So I talked to Mr. Lee and he says the meeting with the new donors will take place two weeks from now. In addition to that he has just connected us to a prospective client that needs a catering affair done. I have the name and number of the person and will call them to get the particulars on what they want and need."

So Bill replies with a smile, "you said something precious to me about our most important affair?

Karlon," this is not that. This is a different affair."

In what seems like 1 day the meeting arrives, but not without a little drama. Morning of meeting, Jerome discovers eggs were not delivered. He brings this to the attention of Karlon.

"What!!!" Karlon yells, "Why did no one tell me we did not have eggs. Who was responsible for checking inventory this morning?"

Jerome replies, "Linda."

Karlon, "Okay Tell Linda go down to the supermarket down the street pick-up 12 dozen eggs and see the store manager and tell him they are for me."

Karlon calls Bill, "What is your ETA?"

Bill replies "About 30 minutes, what up, you got in trouble?"

Karlon, "Nothing serious, I got it if it's going to take you that long."

Karlon announces to staff, "It's time to start setting up the dining hall. Get all the hot foods in first and make sure they are in the warmers set the tables and do what needs to be done you guys know how this goes this is a very important function so I want everything in its proper place. These people will be coming in the side door so let's keep the door to the deli closed I want very few interruptions and I really don't want people to see who is in there maybe some celebrities so don't act surprised just be respectful. If there are any questions regarding the food see Jerome and Bill. We have about one and a half hours could be for people may start showing up so that's it.

Approximately one hour after that Karlon walks into the hall to see final preparations being finished and he says "wow this looks great good job." This looks great if I didn't know you guys I will be impressed." Just after that bill comes in behind Karlon and reiterates how nice the hall looks,

"They did a good job in there bill says."

Karlon replies, "Yeah this is first class we are ready for them now, are you good? Karlon asked?"

Bill. "Yeah I'm ready that's all let's get this going." So Karlon and Bill go to the side door and wait for cars to start pulling in. 10 minutes pass by and the first limo pulls in. Before that car is parked another limo pulls in behind it. After the cars park the first person to come out is Michael Strahan of the New York Giants. The next person to come out is Mr. Lee. After these two guys greet each other in the parking lot they come to the door and Bill and Karlon greet them.

Karlon, "Hey Mr. Lee how are you you're looking pretty sharp there buddy how's everything?"

Mr. Lee replies, "Hey man I'm good what I tell you about that mister stuff we still good so keep it 100 man.

Karlon, "Hello Mr. Strahan nice to meet you glad you could take some time out to come talk with us today." Just as Karlon invites them inside a few more cars pull up into the parking lot and

Karlon said to Bill," why don't you greet these guys and I will deal with Lee and Mr. Strahan." Why don't you guys make yourself comfortable, you can check out the food or have a seat at the table and read the menu that we have made just for this function so you can see what we have available. Just as Karlon says that a few more guys come in that he does not recognize.

Karlon says, "To Lee I don't know who these guys are I will go and introduce myself."

Lee says you can do that but I will introduce you to everybody at the same time once they are all here.

At that time Karlon look up near the door and there's a gentleman standing there by himself with his hands in his pocket just standing there looking over the room. Karlon thinking to himself I know this face I just can't place the name as he walked toward him trying to recognize him before he gets there. And just as he draws near to the gentleman and reaches out his hand to greet him the name comes to him Sean Puffy Combs is in the building. Trying to be professional

Karlon introduces himself and says, Thanks for coming Mr. Combs I appreciate your time, make yourself comfortable we will get started once everyone is here I'm pretty sure there are some faces you recognize. So after a few minutes

Lee address the group. "It looks to me we are all here so let's compose ourselves and I will introduce all that are here and we can get busy.

First, the owner of this establishment Bill Graves, next to him 11 the person we are here to listen to Karlon Brooks, over starting left is lawyers for the new community Jim Davis and Orlando Simmons, next there's Michael Bennett, Antonio Pierce, Carl Banks, Sean P Combs, Charles S Dutton, we also have. Mr. Joe Cotton and James Douglas. At the next table is Real Estate Company the Hollerand Bros. Next is New Jersey real estate man John Jackson, another table full of The Black National Bank of New Jersey. Finally two men I respect very much Mr. Fred Parrish and Terrance Mills.

Now that I have introduced everyone I will state to Mr. Brooks and the New Community we are donors that have met and discussed how we wish to help you and your cause. We have been very impressed with what you are doing and have done so far that we have come together to help. Now what we would like to know from you is now that our help is at your disposal what would be your plans and how much time and effort can you devote to it"

Karlon stands and says,

"first I would like to thank you all for your time and interest in the New Community, God will bless you all for any and all contributions whether it be time, effort or financial, trust me it will be put to good use. I will say my first plans are to raise awareness of the New Community even more, in doing that we can raise the ability to help the community even more. My plans are to stretch out and help more communities, the more help and contributions we receive the more we can spread the help to the communities. As far as my time and effort is concerned, I know you are all aware that I do have job responsibilities with Mr. Bill G. As manager of his deli. And have been doing my job and New Community work from my office there at the deli. Obviously this has caused some concern with Mr. Graves

Board And The Bank

But we have been working through it. I have been devoting my personal time to both my job and New Community. It is hard to say what I can do not knowing just how much is available to me, and I don't want to take my contributors for granted.

Carl Banks stands and says Mr Brooks

." Karlon interrupts him to say, "Ok look I was told we are going to be informal and use first names, Mr. Brooks makes me feel old."

"O k Karlon, "he continues, As we have already discussed some of these issues all ready, what we will tell you is you pretty much have a blank check, however your financial request will take some approving, depending on the amount. One issue is your available time. What would it take to have you devote your efforts full-time to this project?

"Honestly" Karlon replies, "The answer to that is I would have to leave The Sandwich Den, and do this as a job full time."

"Well Karlon" Mr. Lee says, "The question is are you ready and willing to do that?"

"Well" Karlon replies, "for a salary equal to or exceeding my current pay the answer is yes. As me and Mr. G have already discussed this possibility. I don't want to leave him high and dry but he knows how passionate I am about the New Communities objective"

. Mr. Dutton asked, "Karlon can you please tell us what is the ultimate objective of the New Community and what will you ultimately hope to accomplish." Well as I have stated previously, the initial goal was to provide a communication link between black business owners, allowing them to register to do business with each other knowing what products and services they provide. And I don't mean just locally I mean nationwide. While that aspect of the new community has grown and it is still growing the new community has branched out to provide more services to the community and I believe that we can do even more with the expansion of public knowledge of what we are doing. The new community has assisted in helping local politicians with their campaigns, and help them get elected to office. I am currently working on a way to help with job searches, too often we are rejected do to race. So just as we are to communicate with products and services we can do the same with job searches within the black community and again I mean nationwide I also would I like to do more work directly in the community with youth programs, such as after school help.

"You sound like you're running for office." says Lee.

Karlon, "No that's not the case and I don't see how I can do that if I am to resign my position at the deli I will no longer have an office."

John Jackson stands to say, "I believe we can do something about that Karlon. We have discussed supplying you with office space in addition to your salary. We realize that you have been making great strides with the New Community and we feel it is very important to our objective that you expand the public's knowledge on what the New Community is all about. In addition to that we also have agreed to supply you with an apartment in the building where your office will be, we also will offer the Sandwich Den a space to rent in the lobby of the building. This building and office space is a contribution by Mr. John Jackson Realty there will be two floors of empty space that will be for you to do with, for the community only.

Karlon replies, "Okay what do I need to do? Is there a contract I need to sign and are there conditions that I need to meet?"

Carl Banks answers the question by saying" the answer to that is nothing we are all doing this voluntarily. Just as you are doing this voluntarily on your own time. So is our involvement. The reason we are supplying you with a salary is because we want you to do this with a full-time effort. As I said the apartment is just a perk offered by Mr. John Jackson.

John Jackson than asks, "ok Karlon is this something you can deal with or not?"

Karlon says, "I am in so let's get started. I already have some ideas for space in the building that can be used for community purposes. Bill stands to say, "Karlon is free to do as he chooses, I have been preparing for the loss of his services,but Karlon and I remain close friends so I am sure I will not miss him we will see each other, he will always be around. I would like to say I plan on talking to Mr. Jackson about the space in the building is offered to me, it does sound like something I would like to do."

Karlon asked, "Ok what about the financial aspect of things?"

Lee says," Actually after talking to Orlando over there it seems your income flow is legal and being recorded properly, we can just keep that as is. We as donors will make our donations as we choose. We will keep going to the public for more. Any large projects will be approved by us. We trust you bro. We will more than likely just have a discussion about it first, because one of us may have questions about what you're trying to accomplish.

"That's fine Karlon says." I do want to start a promotional campaign, with tee shirts, buttons window stickers and a national insignia that will be recognized. I will look to our website for members that will volunteer to do administrative work for me here in the office. I will also look for volunteer teachers to help students after school with a homework program for the community I wish to start."

Q Mr. Dutton stands to say," I think we have covered good ground here today. We can now bring this meeting to an unofficial close, we can socialize for a while to grab some grub, and we can always communicate online or by phone if more conversations are needed.

Karlon stands to say, "I am glad and honored to have met everyone and glad we have accomplished foundation for a new version of a NEW COMMUNITY.

Karlon walks over to Mr Jackson and says" I appreciate your contribution Sir and would like some time to talk with you about my thoughts for the office and building space that is available". Mr. Jackson replies, "yes sir I would like you to come to my house in Colonia so we can have a comfortable conversation." Just as Karlon acknowledges Mr. Jackson Carl Banks comes up from behind him to say "we need to make a schedule because we have some meetings we would like for you to attend with players. We also have more TV time for you to promote the New Community for support. So it's best that you get a schedule for the next two months so you don't over obligate yourself."

a couple of days after the meeting Karlon and Bill sit in the office to discuss new Arrangements.

Bill, "Well I knew this day was coming because of the success of the new community."

Karlon replies, "Well this will not end our relationship we've been friends and brothers for years and if you accept the space for store in the lobby we will still be close. I will always be available in case you need me regardless of whether I'm working for you or not.

After my meeting with John Jackson my office will be in the lobby, the basement rooms has been set aside for New Community use for whatever I deem to use them for. My apartment is going to be right over my office on the second floor. Samira said after seeing the apartment, she loves it, she especially loves the fact that here is a washing machine and dryer in the apartment. She cannot wait to move. She loves that we have all the room we need. I am going to New York to speak at the NFL players union meeting, just to advertise to other players what's going on with the New Community. They also have me recording an interview that will be put on the news or something for more New Community advertisement. I'm now working on an update to the website to inform members of the new businesses changes and looking for a national logo for buttons and posters and tee-shirts. We have more members running for positions in their communities. By showing up in big numbers at political functions, it gives us more recognition, especially if our members win. I'm also looking for volunteers to work the business office and teachers to help with students and the after work student program. We do have some time because the office needs to be furnish by Mr. Jackson and Company and I need to get my furniture moved into my new apartment. and while all that's been done I can still be helping Bill until the office is ready to be open."

After a month's time Karlon has moved into the apartment and has got a full house of volunteer workers. In the office, he could not have a more trusted crew, including his sister Karien and his girlfriend Samira, for school work and student help. Recruiting a school principal a school vice principal a school counselor and two teachers from local schools to volunteer with the program. After an initial review with them Karien and Samirra will set up the office in order for people to come in for help and express Community problems. After school program crew will start advertising in local schools the help they will be given to the students. Karlon after seeing the offices became so enthused he wanted to come up with names for the rooms so the community room will now be known as THE C.A.Ŕ. Community Assistance Room. School work program will be known as CLAP, Community Learning Assistance Program. After all that Karlon goes to do his speech to NFL players union. In addition to that a commercial will be made from it. So Karlon decides to make a surprise announcement. Stating that in addition to the community services now being provided in Irvington, NJ, that more New Community centers will be furnished to do the same across the country.

Karlon arrived at Giants stadium to talk to not just Giants rookies, but all NFL rookies and second-year players on the East Coast.

"Good afternoon gentlemen," Karlon says, "I understand we have second-year and rookies here. First of all, I congratulate you on your accomplishments in becoming professional players. This is something that should not be taken lightly. I want you to know that there are many difficulties being in the Limelight. It will take a toll on your professional and private life. I understand you guys that are here are interested in giving back to your community, I am here to show you a way that will make it convenient for you and show you how your donations will help in a broad manner of ways. Some are interested in helping with education in the community some are interested and helping with housing in the community, I'm here to tell you that the new community can help in all of these areas with your donations. Yes we are asking for money from your end of the process to change our communities. But there are others that will help in other ways. We have black lawyers, to help those that can't afford it. We have black doctors that can give free examinations for adults, and free treatment for children. Black judges, we have black real estate owners that can give fair and decent housing to our people. These people will give their time and professions in order to help the community in this process. We also have construction companies that will help in the process refelting the housing in the community. But most of all a lump sum of help will come from the communities themselves with volunteers donating their time and labor to help you build their own community. We as blacks fill we don't get a fair shake and a lot of these areas so now that we have black owned businesses helping us so we can make better progress. My vision is for us to come full circle in this process so that we can become self-sufficient. I know you guys are stars from some areas across the country and trust me we are trying to build community centers in as many cities as we can. This will allow us and you the opportunity to help in the city of your choice or just to our general cause, which would help and all cities. And trust me there are other ways you can help. You can make personal appearances in areas of your choice, to give motivation to the local community, who also give their own time, money, and effort to help. I'm also aware you guys have been given the speech about staying out of trouble, trust me this cannot be understated. I know you guys are not children please when you're out in public have a bodyguard or chaperone, when you're out in the club have more than one. It is better to have some functions at home where you can have more witnesses in case of trouble. Please keep your eyes open or the Flusees, you know who they are don't act like you don't they are out there for one thing only and that's to get you caught up. When out in public in case of intoxication your bodyguards should be ordered to get you home. And in extreme cases you should have at least one guard license to carry firearms, depending on the size of the function or crowd maybe more than one. Remember you are worth a lot of money, protect yourself at all times, some people are jealous, and will attempt to bring you down for absolutely no reason at all. And when it comes to drugs I know you guys know better. If you need drugs to have a good time then you're not having a good time. Instead of using P E D'S, just workout more and better, why jeopardize your health and career which is your money. And by the way, don't ask me who my favorite team is, I don't want to get beat up as I try to get out of here. Thanks for your time guys, have a great season."

. So Karlon puts together a new commercial to be broadcast. The commercial will include information of the new community how it started and where is at the present time. Karlon ask for help from our sport star actors and other wealthy people that can contribute to the financial aid of the new community and the programs they want to implement to help our people. Karlon talks about initiation of the website and how it was geared to help black business owners connect with one another. He also talked about how the website helped. The community as far as keeping the wealth of black money in our own community he also spoke about how the website grew in order to help political members gain office. Members of the new community got together for fundraisers and attending rallies to help our new community members gain office. He talked about how through donations and volunteer work we were able to open our first community room. He talked about the function of the community room and how it was set up to assist people with problems in the community. He talked about how through volunteers donating their time we were able to set up a program for students with after-school programs. He talked about and asked for more volunteers from our people such as lawyers to help people that can't afford them to volunteer legal information. He asked for realtors and banking institutions to set up plans for low income people to help with home ownership. he talked about how many of our black millionaire actors and sports athletes are always looking for ways to give back to the community and shows that this is a great way to do just that. Once the commercial edited, it hits the tv screen in no time at all.

Karlon awakes the next day with Samira rushing him to the TV to see his commercial. Walking to his car as he heads out to work with people calling his name. Going to the deli with messages, Jerome and Linda telling him girls have been coming to the store asking for and about him. Linda says she tells the girls Karlon is spoken for and has a family so don't make any plans for him.

Karlon laughs and said, "I'm here because I promised Bill I would be here until the C.A.R (Community Assistance Room) is ready to open which will be this coming Monday." The website is full of request for Community Rooms. Then Karlon notices an email from Newark's mayor Cory Booker, so Karlon decides to call him instead. After getting thru the mayors screening,

Karlon, "hello mayor this is Karlon Brooks, you emailed me so I decided to call to avoid any emails spies, Karlon laughs."

Mayor, "Yes Mr. Brooks I wanted to ask some questions about the community rooms. Why is there not one in Newark?"

Karlon replies, "Well, Mr. Mayor due to the fact that we just opened the first one, the rooms are being placed on the need for one in the city not necessarily based on the size of the city. Anyone in Newark looking for services can come to the Irvington office until we see the need to put one in your city to make it more feasible. What you can do is put a memo to your constituents in your city to raise money for an office or have someone donate office space for the community room and we will do the rest. If you do this much, you should also ask for volunteers for office work and teachers to help with students from your local community schools in the after school program.

The Mayor responds, ".Ok Mr. Brooks I understand. I have much faith in the people of Newark and they will come through. I will get back to you when progress is made.

Karlon says, Just to put you up to date Mr. Mayor we are also looking for a national logo for the New Community to use for buttons, posters and etc. Anything you or your friends can do would be of help.

Mayor, "Ok thanks for the info. If we can do something to help we will. Thanks for calling Karlon I appreciate it."

"No problem sir." Karlon says. Karlon steps out of the office and into deli to get lunch,as he sits down customers are coming to him to ask questions, or just to say hello and congrats on your success. His popularity is not allowing for much privacy. So he steps back into the office to eat just as he does.

Bill comes in and ask, "Why are you eating in the office when there is space out there for you to eat."

Karlon replies, "It may be room but not much privacy, it seems as if everyone wants to speak to me that never spoke to you before, women are offering their numbers and underwear," and they both laugh. Yes bill says your popularity is actually causing an issue. Karlon says well my office opens Monday I would like for you to come to see how things are going and maybe offer some mentorship. But for right now I'm here with you until I go home. The new apartment is shaping up well, we have plenty of room, and Samira is doing a great job decorating and setting things up. So I'll be there most of the weekend, hope to see you Monday. Bill replies ok later. So Karlon does just that spends most of the weekend at home keeping Karlon Jr. out of the way while Samira does most of the decorating at home.

Monday is here and the office opening goes on without any hoopla. Karien is answering telephone call regarding Community issues while Samira is setting up schedules for students for the after school programs and volunteer teachers for the students. Karlon contacts James Meyers who is running with Mr. Kasim Reed for the mayor's seat. James who will be vice--mayor is a longtime member because of his owning two delicatessens. Karlon explains to James it would be better if he could get Mr. Kasim to join TNC (The New Community) it would validate us supporting both of you. We can send you guys tees, buttons, and posters, for your next rally. Get back to me latter ok,? Karlon asked. Ok dude hang on I'll holla at you latter.

Karlon back on the website is reading an idea from a member on more things that TNC can do to help the people, such as job hunting and real estate. So Karlon puts out a question to the board members on what we can do real estate wise to help. After that he puts out a memo to local members to advertise job openings they are looking to fill on the website. In addition to that TNC will post these openings in and around the community for local job hunters to see. Do to the increased popularity of what TNC can and is willing to do, more ad more people are coming to the C.A.R community assistance room, Karlon brings in more volunteer workers to assist in the community room. A couple that also lives in the building agrees to volunteer to the community room. Dennis Thompson and his wife Belinda will help with community services.

A couple of days later Karlon puts out a call to Mr. John Jackson to ask about real estate help for low income buyers or people with low credit ratings.

Karlon, "Mr. Jackson, I was wondering if there was any word on the real estate issues I asked about?"

Mr. Jackson, "Yes Karlon we have had our own meeting and have come up with ideas that would help, but we need more assistance from other real estate and financial institutions in order to help on a large scale.

À replies, "I understand Mr. Jackson I actually feel we need more people in other prominent positions to help such as lawyers and doctors and other sports figures that can lend financial help to our cause, maybe this is what we need to for more. So what I'm going to do is put out a request to the board to do a commercial about the new community and our progress of what we are about,and the assistance that we need of more volunteers and financial donations to help our cause. After Karlon speech hits the internet and website and commercials Karlon gets a call from Mr. Lee. Hey bro. what's up?

Karlon replies, "You know the deal man, I'm trying to do my thing man."

Lee says, "Yea man you working hard and we can see that, but I'm thinking for you to fall back a little bit and let it grow for a while and after that you can see maybe what adjustments might need to be made. So other than that how are you doing? If you need an ear to lean on you can always come over give me a holler and we can talk. Karlon replies, "yeah man I think that's a good idea I would like to do just that, so if you're available I'll come over tomorrow and holler at you about some things that's on my mind." So just as tomorrow comes Karlon sets out on track to Lee's office. But before Karlon arrives Lee gets a phone call, "Hey Lee its Karlon, I'm stuck on the highway I had car problems my car needs to be towed I will be delayed in getting there, or maybe even have to turn back."

Lee replies, "Hey man I can send a car for you to bring you here and return you home after our meeting if you like."

Karlon replies, "Yeah okay that's cool." Karlon sits in the car waiting for tow truck and just as the tow trucks arrives so does a limousine pulled up behind it. Karlon get to Lee's office and says, "man I'm expecting a cab and you send a limousine to pick me up, a little over-the-top don't you think?"

Lee replies with a laugh and says, "that's what I had available don't sweat it. So Lee says, look first things first do you need a car? We don't need you getting stuck on the highway In order to get to meetings that may be important.

Karlon answers, "At the present time I'm going to have to say yeah I do need a car I'm not looking for a handout though not looking for you to buy me no Benz or anything high class. And

Lee says, "I don't think you have to worry about that. That's not going to happen but I can set you up with a easy loan at a dealership of a friend of mine's for you to get something better and more dependable. Karlon said, "okay that's cool I can do that."

Lee, "Okay what's going on what do we need to talk about?"

Karlon replies, "Man, it's just the pressure of what's going on, and what we're doing is beginning to become a lot for me".

Lee says, "You know what I thought just that, it's the reason why I said for you to fall back a little bit and just let things grow we're pushing a little too hard.

Karlon, "on a more personal level it looks like I will be getting married soon, I'm thinking of officially popping the question the ring is already in hand.

Lee says, "Aww man that's the easy part, you got a good job good pay, don't overthink it if you love her and she loves you let it do what it do. After the heart to heart talk, Karlon decides to take Samira with him car shopping, he picks out a dodge sedan and does a test drive,in the process he tells Samira to check the size of the glove box, Samira opens the box and says, ``there's a little box in here,

Karlon says, "Open it up," as she does, she begins to get the surprise, and smiles like she never has before.

Karlon says," You are the best partner, lover, and friend that I have ever had in my life, will you marry me?"

Samira wipes her eyes and says, "Yes, you know I always wanted us to get married.

Karlon says, "yes but I had to ask officially. It comes with a nice car." She smiles, and asked, "Can we go tell my mother she is sick, maybe this will brighten her up.?"

Karlon replies, "yes, let's close this car deal and head over there." Karlon and Samira cheerfully make their family notification and return home to get the final approval of one last member, one year old Karlon Jr. After a blissful family night Karlon and Samira's first duty of the next day is to announce their wedding day. December 15th. Karlon decides to have the details and plans to the wedding handled by his sister Karien who with her organization called (We Do That) does wedding planning and decorations. Karlon decides to relax from media and website promotions and let things grow as it was suggested to him by Lee.

National Transition

Karlon gets back to work in his office reading emails and website updates. Karlon is reading that more cities and communities are opening their own Community rooms. Karlon is also reading website updates that more celebrities' sports stars and other wealthy black businessmen are joining and registering for membership in the new community. Karlon gets an email from Lee saying he is getting more black stars making large commitments to The New Community some making large donations and some making commitments of volunteering time and professional advice or skills. Karlon decides to make some calls such as calling Mr. Charles Dutton and Mr. John Jackson who have left messages for him to speak to

. Karlon speaks to Mr. Dutton and says, "yes we are getting more black professionals looking to volunteer time and professional skills such as lawyers and doctors, to the point where we may need to put them in their own group to decide what things they want to volunteer to the new community, and how they want to distribute their value on a national level."

Dutton responds," this sounds good to me, just realizing how many are volunteering. If we are getting that many volunteering their time and skills and knowledge yes I think we should group them so that they can decide how to spread their value on a national level. So we can do the same with Dr.'s and real estate people. Teachers and banking institutions can be kept on the local level, because there are so many differences depending on what part of the country you are in."

Karlon, "So Mr. Dutton you can implement these changes with the board and I will inform members on the website."

Dutton replies, "Okay Karlon, Thanks for the call I will speak to you later on any updates as they come." So Karlon puts a call to Mr. John Jackson to inform him of his conversation with Mr Dutton and let him know he can do the same with the real estate people on a national level. This will be the answer to a question that we asked in a previous conversation

Mr. Jackson says, "Ok, Mr. Brooks that's fine I will put things in motion on my end."

Karlon, "Ok John talk to you later sir."

Next day Karlon gets a call from Newark mayor Mr. Booker.

"Hello Mr. Brooks" Mr. Booker says, "I'm calling you to update you with Newark's progress, we have actually started three community centers. Because of the size of my city we found it more plausible to have more than one.

Karlon replies, "That's fine Mr. Mayor, I understand you need to have the community centers more local in the community, as long as they are registered in the new Community website. I am calling on another matter Karlon, I wanted you to know that I am planning to run for state senator."

Karlon replies, "Well congratulations on that sir. I'm pretty sure you want the support of the new community, but I do not see that you have personally registered as a member. I know that you have people on your staff that are members. But if you want the support of the new community to run for an office, it will be more plausible for you to be a member yourself. After you do that, I can post it on the website and we can help you with your campaign.

Ok says Mr. Booker, "I will." Karlon sits and stares at his computer for a while after that conversation with the mayor. So he puts in a call to Mr. Jim Davis.

"Hey Jim," Karlon shouts.

"Yoo man what's up" Jim replies.

"Karlon says, "I just called to get an update of the numbers. Members, money and community centers

. Jim replies, "You realize we are a non-profit organization. Yes Karlon replies. Well with the money that we have, and what's coming in lately, we need to start spending it, so we don't seem to be hoarding these dollars. Regulations require us to do something with it in order to keep our status.

"Ok hit me" Karlon says.

Jim replies, "$800,000 in cash, 125,000 total members 40 centers including ones just being registered. We are spreading across the country, but we are surprisingly week in some areas.

"Yes" Karlon replies, "we need to be known and spread nationally. You look at that money, and have the urge to buy a new car?

"No" Karlon says, "Actually I just bought a car. Not brand new, but I needed something dependable.

Jim laughs, "bad timing" and laughs again. "You could have brought a brand new joint and put a new community sticker on the side. "Hell no" Karlon yells, "people would see right through that, it would be stealing from the very people I'm trying to help. Not going to do the white people thing, somewhere down the line it will pop up. I'm not going to put myself or the new community in that position.

I was just informed that Cory Booker is going to run for the senate. So after his membership is registered we can spend some on his campaign. We need to add something to our services or add something to community rooms, but what we do for one goes for all nationally. You have any ideas?"

"No" Jim replied, "but I'm sure an idea will come up."

"Ok look," Karlon said, "I'll talk to you later. I'm going to squeeze my brain to see if I can come up with an idea." Karlon

sits in his office just thinking of what can be done to make the new community go bigtime. Karlon puts in a call to Lee.

"Hey how are you?" Karlon asked,"

Lee, "Mr. Karlon what up my dude?"

Well Mr. Lee, I got your email. And I'm not satisfied with the numbers I see. And there are areas that we are very weak in. You guys said I should chill a bit but we still have some issues to deal with as far as getting more national recognition.

Lee says, "Ok so you want to go national?"

Karlon responds, "Yes, as a matter of fact, I do. I think it should be known that we are national not just in certain communities. We need to be spread out evenly across the country not just in certain spots. And as a matter of fact, I think we should present ourselves nationally as in changing the name to say we are national. And we should incorporate the word black in our name too. To amplify that we are here to help black people. We need a meeting, maybe a conference call. Let's get that together in maybe a couple of days. What do you think?"

Lee answers," Well I don't think we necessarily need to change the name. The name new community has been out there for a while, we just need to do as you say and promote ourselves better in other areas, however I do understand the effects of changing the name to reflect nationally black, let's get this conference call together and see what other people may think".

Karlon says, "Ok let's make this call in 3 days, give them time to put some time aside for the call, it may be a long one."

Three days later Karlon now having the ability to conference call from his office, no longer has to travel to Mr. Lee's office to do so. Starts the call at 2:00 pm. Most of the brain trust were present.

Karlon starts by saying, "As always I love and appreciate your time and efforts to the new community, I wanted to update you on the current status of the new community, and my thoughts on where we should go from here. Although our numbers continue to grow. At last count membership was 347,600. Our available funds are, $800,000. I look at these numbers from where we started and I smile. But when I think about where I want us to be and where we should be, my face curls up to a frown. I would like us to be bigger and better. At this point I would like to know if there are any thoughts or ideas on this matter?"

"Pearce here," he says boldly. "I believe in what we are doing. I feel we need more support from the community. The community needs to know that we are here to help them. Unfortunately most people don't join or participate until they feel it's going to help them personally. I'm willing to help whatever direction we go. Karlon, "Thanks, "I appreciate your candor, and your dedication. Karlon says. "I think they need to feel us in their heart, and need to see us as leaders out front. They need to know who is leading them and have faith in that leader. A lot of people in the group feel I should be out front, and I disagree with that, because the public doesn't know me. They know Mr. Lee. They know Charles S Dutton. Having people of their stature would gather the confidence of the people. Anyone else?"

"Yes, this is Orlando Simmons. Because I'm close to the numbers I agree with what you said previously, that what we have financially will not be enough to do what we want to do on a national level. In order to be strong we need to be financially strong. Obviously if we are going to make changes, we need financial changes."

Yes thanks Orlando," Karlon says. "That makes good sense hopefully are financial changes are increases. I'm sure we all agree with that. So, we need more money and a prominent person to stand out front. We need to make the people feel that what we're trying to do will help them personally. So if the people we do not want to be out front we need an influx of more people to choose from to stand in that position. We need more of our influential people to step up financially to help us even if it's just volunteering time skills and knowledge such as lawyers doctors law enforcement and sports stars to step up and help us in a way that will be financially and with celebrities backing us up. My idea was to change the name of the new community to something I feel that what make our people more interested, feel more stronger about it and have more faith that what we're doing will help them. So the name I came up with is National Black Community. I think this will make all people feel that we are on a national level not just the local communities, the word black should bring a feeling that we are here to help our people. I understand that initials N B C cannot be used. So I came up with the idea if we use an abbreviation it will be National BC or T N B C. Mr. Brooks a voice rings out,

"Carl Banks here, I remember hearing a request for a logo for posters and things of that nature have they been done and do we need to redo such logo?"

"actually no" Karlon replied, "A request was put out for a logo but nothing came back in return that we can use, so nothing needs to be redone. So at this time I would ask that you members send in your thoughts on changing the name and what you think the abbreviation should be for the logo and posters and things of that nature. So I'm also going to put this on the website for other members to vote on and we will go from there. so before we discontinue this communication, I will ask that we search for more names and people to put out front and search for more financial coverage and more help with volunteers and celebrities and judges and doctors and lawyers and law enforcement people to join the new community because we are going national people and there's no doubt about that."

So after a week of watching the voting on the website, and realizes that the name that was chosen THE NATIONAL BLACK COMMUNITY. the fact that this was chosen allows us to use the anagram T N B C without any problems of infringement on NBC. new names that have joined TNBC are names that will allow us to put them out front and represent us in their local areas. Charles S. Dutton will be and area representative on the West Coast. also joining us on the west coast Cochran Law Firm. on the East Coast the Reverend Al Sharpton will be a spokesman for TNBC. representing Us in the south will be Senator Edward Brooke and the Reverend Jesse Jackson will also be a spokesman for TNBC. Some athletic sports stars have made large donations and agreed to make appearances in support of TNBC. The president of the NBA players union Chris Paul, along with him are LeBron James, Dewayne Wade, and Carmelo Anthony who will also speak on behalf of TNBC. Michael Bennett from the NFL and

Curtis Granderson will be our MLB REP. We have gathered many new members for support and have made a major breakthrough financially which will allow us to do things previously only dreams of.

As I don't want to speak to far ahead I can tell you our very next step is to include homeless centers in every city of a community room. We are trying to do what we can to help our people but things will need to be done one step at a time. Being that funds are available the construction of homeless shelters has begun and have created more jobs in the community. Job search programs will be available for homeless. We are putting out requests for grooming services for homeless victims from neighborhood barber shops and Beauty parlors. We are now putting out request for artists to make a moniker for posters, signs, and buttons. We rely on our community members for volunteer services because what we do is for the community.

We will now turn our attention to helping our member Corey Booker in his quest for a New Jersey senator's seat. We have shown our support at one of his political speeches, and he mentioned TNBC as a major supporter to his campaign. By doing that, those that don't know now want to know who is the TNBC. At his interview on CNN Mr. Booker again was asked about TNBC, Mr. Booker explained the group's purpose was to assist the black community in ways not otherwise available. Noting that the group was previously known as The New Community. And changed the name to represent the expansion of the group to a national level. And when asked who is the leader of the group, MR. Booker began to run off a who's who list of prominent people. Saying TNBC is governed by a board of these people not one person. But he did say the origin of the organization was led by a young man by the name of Karlon Brooks. This gentleman was just a deli manager and came up with the idea from his experience in being turned down for a small business loan.

After this interview Karlon was sought out by CNN, Karlon meets with board via conference call to ask if there are any objections to him meeting with CNN or ABC., or any restricted info he should hold back on. No one had any objections or interview with CNN first. And for cosmetic sake he took Samira with him, and for the first time he introduced her as his wife.

"Hello, I'm John Rollins and this is CNN COMMUNITY NEWS I'm here with Karlon Brooks and his wife Samira. Mr. Brooks is a community leader that has bonded his community together and has set in motion benefits for the community through people volunteering services and time.

Mr. Brooks I understand there is more to your plan in motion, but I will let you explain it.

"Hello Mr. Rollins," Karlon says, "first I would like to thank CNN for this opportunity to come on and explain what TNBC is all about. I would not consider myself a community leader, there is more to this than myself, all the business owners are a big part in this, they are all leaders. We did first start in the community by having local businesses communicate with each other through a website to advertise their products and services. The reason for this was so that black business could do business with each other. This would benefit black business and the community. This has also strengthened the community to have a stronger voice politically. We have made a difference in some political races all over the country. We are now focusing on real estate. Trying to make decent housing for low income families. We are looking to build or rebuild structures in vacant areas to revitalize the community. We have Realtors and bankers to finance these operations. We are still leaning on donations from our leaders, sports stars, and celebrities.

So I am putting out a plea to our black millionaires to give back to the community. We have sports stars making 10 to 20 million a year. Some actors making 100 million a movie. High earning black judges and doctors. Rich real estate Moguls and banking financiers that can contribute to the community that they came from. We are trying to help our people that are under privileged. People that need help getting on their feet. We are trying to get better opportunities for better housing, opportunities for better jobs and education for our youth. These are things that we don't get equal opportunity for, so we are going to do it for ourselves. One of the ideas is to rebuild an entire community. This is something that can be done in multiple areas. And I mean complete communities including stores shops, laundromats, even entertainment areas such as movie theaters and restaurants. I am also hoping that maybe a large employer such as Production Company or warehouse or large mall can be brought to the area to bring in more jobs for people living in the community.

Mr. Rollins interrupts to ask,

"Mr. Brooks you seem to have large ideas for TNBC, but do you have a plan in place to get it all done?"

"Well sir," Karlon replies, "the answer to that is yes. We are made up in group's that will handle specific aspects of all projects. We have people that are contributing from many aspects of life, and professions. construction companies, Realtors, bankers, but one of our largest areas of help will come from people that just plain want to contribute in any way they can, whether it be monetary or sacrificing time and labor. Some of our people realize the point of our cause and just want to help in any way they can, and you can't put a value on that. They know that the point of what we're doing will help them in the long run and they want to see that this goes through."

"Okay Mr. Brooks," says

John Rollins, "my next question is what is the next step for TNBC? "Well John" Karlon replies, "We will get together to discuss our finances and projects. We will decide what projects we have enough money to allocate to. We will not start a project unless we have allocated enough money to finish it. I would like to give you an example of what we do in the TNBC. We have been approached by a church in the neighborhood that we are working in, and they have asked us to rebuild their structure. Regardless of personal religious beliefs we have agreed to do so. However, we are not doing this out of the finances of the TNBC They are providing financing and materials however we have enough volunteers to do this labor for free. What you don't see is some of the guys that are volunteering their time to do construction projects are getting hired by Contractors & construction companies because of the work that they are doing."

Mr. Rollins, "okay my next question is for the misses, I understand you do have some function administrative wise can you elaborate on what you do?"

Samira says, "Yes sir Mr. Rollins, I work in the office with my sister-in-law Karien Brooks and volunteers, on our after-school study program. We also handle community situations with business owners and residence with whatever issues they may have.

Rollins, "Very nice guys, you seem to be very organized. But let me ask if there are any drawbacks? Have you had any problems with people not understanding or disagreeing with what you're program is doing?"

Karlon replies, "Actually no."

Mr. Rollins, "then asked, "What I'm trying to get to is the fact that your program is to help black people get equal opportunity to housing and employment opportunities, are you getting any drawback from white people? Are you also offering opportunities for them?"

"Well Mr. Rollins," Karlon says," We are not excluding anyone. We have not turned away anyone due to race. Whether it be in our online membership or applying for applications for work or housing, or volunteering their time or money. The truth is at this time I believe we are close to 1 million total members, I cannot tell you how many of them are white, or any other race. Because we have not asked that question on any of our applications.

We will not use the same racist or Prejudice policies against other people that have been used against our people for years. Bottom line is our goal is to help our black people get fair opportunities at jobs and housing. But we are here to help any and all people. "Well, Mr. Brooks, "I will again say that I am impressed with what you're doing and as you have said with your members and applicants I am looking to see it come to its reality. Well, ladies and gentlemen, I'm John Rollins and that's our report for today on the TNBC." After leaving the studio Karlon's next order of business is to call upon the board to hear what they thought of the interview. After a few hours Karlon joins in on a conference call that is already in progress. "Hello gentlemen this is Karlon, I'm just joining in and I'm sure you guys have some retorts about my interview today so let me have it."

"Hey Karlon this is Charles we have been talking for approximately 1/2 hour already and I'm pretty sure I speak for most of the guys on the board and yes we have all been busy on phone calls since your interview was over. And I mean to say that in a positive way.

"Karlon, this is J. Davis and yes we have been busy on phone calls and I have been busy taking in more donations and things have gotten to a point that they have never been before. Some extremely large numbers have been coming through."

Karlon says, "So am I to believe that we will get the go-ahead on more projects?"

Mr. Davis answers, "I believe that's a yes, I think that we should expedite some projects in order to give a good outlook on what we are doing. What I think we need is a signature project something large or special to get national attention and the public eye and interest. So let's call on a couple of people for some ideas especially Mr. Jackson."

Karlon then says, "You know what? I just got an idea. We talked about building an entire community before. Stores, housing, laundromat a commercial business such as a mall movie theater and some other businesses that can bring in opportunity for jobs. So let's get some numbers on that and propose it to the board and see what we can do. Let's get Mr. Jackson and the Hudlin Brothers to see what areas they can find that we can use to revitalize. We may need to get some cities architects to draw up plans for structures and buildings and businesses. We can also draw in some housing separate but close by the businesses. I will get Karien and her crew to contact some businesses that may want to join in this venture." Karlon gets together with Mr. Jackson and they decide to take a ride around town to look at some areas that might be good for the plan. After doing this they decide to get a map of an overview of the city and look at it that way that might be easier to see prospective areas for revitalization. After doing this for a couple of days they have come to a decision on an area that may best.

. Karlon says to Mr. Jackson, Look I don't think you guys need me for the next part, just get an architectural drawing of a perspective plan and get some figures to present to the board as far as numbers. Mr. Jackson reaches out to a Mr. Lewis Johnson for architectural design. And after 2 weeks Mr. Johnson comes back with his rendering of the revitalized area. Mr. Jackson takes his rendering to the board and ask them for financial approval and a budget for the plan. After a couple of days Mr. Johnson gets a call from the board telling him that the plan has been approved with an open budget. Mister Johnson hops on the phone immediately and calls Karlon. Mr. Johnson, "I'm calling to tell you the plan has been approved by the board for the new revitalize area. But the surprise in the deal is that there is an open budget meaning spend what you have to do to get the job done. Any extremes will be red flagged,"

Karlon replies. "Fine that's great news, what we need to do now is to complete all projects that are in the works, and work on this project only. We may need to put out a request for extra workers in order to keep production in a good time frame." Karlon asks "how are we doing with businesses for the mall?"

Mr. Johnson replies, "we have multiple request for pharmacies we have an auto repair, we have a cleaners obviously we have multiple requests for Chinese food restaurants wishing to occupy a spot. We have a request from McDonald's and Wendy's. We also have a shoe store complete for mens and women sneakers and shoes. However I did just get a request for a pool parlor which I believe we will not approve. Obviously that's asking for trouble so we will stay away from that. We will have one men's clothing store and one ladies clothing store to keep a good balance. In addition we will have a separate building for a Walmart Superstore including groceries." At the office of John Jackson a call comes in from a reporter of the Star Ledger newspaper.

"Mr. Jackson my name is Dave Adams I'm calling to get some info on your company buying a large amount of property in the city of Irvington Would you care to comment or elaborate on this information?"

"Well Mr. Adams I'm not sure why this is newsworthy but yes we are buying land and property in the city of Irvington to do some construction on housing."

Mr. Adams, "Well Mr. Jackson at this point it seems to be a considerably large amount of land and property that's why it came to my attention and seems to be newsworthy depending on the purpose of the construction. Mr. Adams asked would you care to elaborate on the purpose of this construction or give us some insight to your company's main goal?"

Mr. Jackson replies. "Without going into too much detail we are constructing a community for low income families."

Mr. Adams then asks, "Just to confirm, you said your building a community?"

MR. Jackson says, "Yes that's all I have for you today, maybe more info will be put out later. Mr. Jackson waste no time bringing his encounter to the attention of his colleges at the next conference call of TNBC board members. Ladies and gents, MR. Jackson says," I've been contacted by the Star Ledger, asking questions about our purchases of property in Irvington I think we need to get in front of this before they start printing what they want about what we are doing. One board member says, maybe we can get Mr. Brooks on CNN again and do an interview to put out what info we want before the Star Ledger comes out with what they want.

"Hello ladies and gents, this is Lee, I can arrange that interview, and I will get on it right away. But in addition to Mr. Brooks I'm thinking that maybe you Mr. Jackson should go along for the interview for info on the purchases of land and construction side of things., Mr. Brooks can you fill them in on our main goal and the procedure of getting all this done.

Mr. Jackson replies, "that's fine with me I have no problem with that.

Lee says, "Ok with that I will put in a call to CNN and get a time frame from Mr. Rollins. He will be surprised that we are requesting the interview this time. First step is to call Karlon Brooks." The next day a ringing phone wakes Karlon in the morning hours.

Hello Karlon says, good morning."

Karlon, this is Lee how are you brother?

Karlon answers, "I'm just waking up, how are you?

"What's up this is Lee" he replies. "Well I needed to inform you we need to schedule an interview with CNN more than likely with John Rollins."

Karlon replies, "Why is that? What do we need to say?"

"Well apparently John Jackson got a phone call from The Star-Ledger inquiring about property TNBC has been buying in the city of Irvington AFTER speaking with the group, we decided to get in front of anything they might print out. Mr. Jackson did confirm to them that we are buying property to build housing. But we don't want them to speculate and start rumors about what we're doing. So this time John will go with you to tell the public about the land and the project we are working on. You will be informing them about the process."

Karlon asks, "Why is building housing an issue?"

Lee answers, "Well because John told them we are building a community.

"Ok then set it up with CNN and let me know, Karlon relies."

Lee then says, "Tell Samira she can come but she won't be on tv, Lee laughs.

"Yea" Karlon says, "She's laughing now because she heard you. Ok holla back Karlon says as he hangs up." Karlon and Samira look at each other and just laugh uncontrollably.

Karlon says to Samira, "I want to get dressed up this time, so I'm considering looking for a new suit to wear, because this interview might be important to the TNBC. I want to look my best. I think we will be addressing more of an audience this time"

.One week later, Karlon and John arrive at CNN to do the interview with Mr. Rollins. As Mr. Rollins approaches

Karlon says, "Mr. Rollins this is John Jackson one of my board members that is the head of the real estate aspect of our operation. `` As they shake hands,

Mr. Rollins says, "relax John this interview is going to be very easy, I'm going to let you do most of the talking my questions will be short and sweet."

That's okay Mr. Rollins John replies, "My answers may be short and sweet too, as they both laugh.

Karlon says to John, "look you know what the info you're to give out and explain?

John answers, "yes, I will give them the process of land purchasing, the businesses that will be on the land, and the distribution of housing.

"You got it" Karlon says. John turned around and asked, "how do I look?"

Karlon replies, "You look like a real estate Tycoon and I look like Karlon Brooks the man about to change the world as we now see it." They both hear a voice say," okay you guys come have a seat on stage and we will get started."

It's John Rollins, he continues by saying, "Welcome, this is CNN neighborhood watch and I'm John Rollins. Today we will speak to someone that we have spoken with in the past, mister Karlon Brooks. We will revisit his organization The New Community which has been renamed The National Black Community. In addition we have John Jackson who is the head of real estate in TNBC. It's my understanding Mister Jackson that the TNBC has brought a lot of property in the city of Irvington And you are here to explain what you as an organization plans to do with this property which I understand is a considerable amount.

"Yes", Mr Rollins. "I'm here to explain why we are buying this property and what we plan to do with it. And the reasoning behind it. To put it simply we are buying land and property to build a community for low and middle-income families. We find that even the working middle-class family has a hard time finding decent housing due to prejudiced decisions made by other real estate groups. What we have done is include the community in helping with construction of this property by way of volunteers. And in the process of doing that we are creating jobs in the construction industry by doing this. Any of the volunteers that work on construction and complete a construction project will be hired and paid for the next project and after. Now during their volunteer times they are trained in safety and covered medically. If they don't have their own insurance, we will cover any injuries or medical issues coming from the construction that they may have. We are working with the city and state on city housing applications and Section 8 applications to make sure that people that have been waiting for housing are appropriately placed in a proper timeline. And yes this a community so we did purchase a large amount of property.

Mr. Rollins says, "If I may interject. You are building a community and I am sure that takes a lot of funding, you have a large company or are funded by external people. Yes again John answers, we are blessed with contributions from celebrities, Sports athletes, doctors lawyers judges and other community minded people that want this project to succeed. We have been soliciting for donations, and volunteers by way of tv advertising, the website, posters in the community and businesses. And pamphlets being passed out. Also once we reached a couple of celebrities and pro athletes the news in those circles travels well."

Mr. Rollins the asked, "Well, John just how long do you think this will all take to finish?"

Mr. Jackson replies, "Well we are not putting any time frame on this project, due to the variable of volunteers. Obviously want to finish the project as fast and efficiently as possible but there are no requirements for the volunteers so this is the variable that affects the timeline. Okay Mr. Brooks "I'm sure you have something to add to the information here." Mr. Rollins asked. "Would you care to remind some of our audience and fill in those that do not know the history of the TNBC?"

Karlon "Thank you, John, I would like to start by saying all of what is being done is by the efforts of our people communicating and volunteering to help each other. I've always heard as a young man how are how our people do not help each other like other nationalities do. I would like to prove those people wrong. And by the progress we are making we are doing just that. The original website that started to help black business owners communicate with other black business owners to publicize their products and services to each other. By doing this we have blacks doing business with blacks in order to help keep the money and prosperity in our own communities. The communication and membership level continue to grow with this website and to the point where it leaked into the community. The community began to grow closer to the point where they got together to pick and promote the leaders they chose to run for office. This led to the forming of the new community organization. Once the organization got together they decided to put their efforts towards real estate for the community. Due to the lack of proper housing for low and middle class income families. In addition to this they started programs in the community such as after school study programs for students that needed extra help. We have gotten volunteers from teachers to help with this effort. We got volunteers from the community to help in the office of the new community organization. It was around this time that we began to get donations from the community. So we legalized ourselves to be a nonprofit organization in order to take these donations legally. It was around this time that I got in touch with mister Lee, and as I said once we got into the celebrity and pro athlete circles once I told Mr. Lee about the goals of our organization and expressed to him that we needed the help of our black rich and famous people in order to get this done. This projects was intended to help all of our people Nationwide and he agreed. For too long our people have been criticized for the lack of effort in helping ourselves. Once this project succeeds we will have put a change in opinion as to the progress of our people. Once he agreed to help, donations began to get often and large. An officers board was formed to approve and suggest projects for the new community to work on. The popularity of the new community and its membership spread nationwide, and we wanted to project to our membership that we represent our people nationally, so therefore we changed the name to the National Black Community. This project will set a new standard of living for our people. All of the apartments will include the top of the line fixtures and appliances. From Studios to 5 bedroom apartments all will be set with dish washers, washer and dryers, master bedroom ensuites, garages, some will have two levels. With all sharing open backyard space. And yes the most modern alarm systems in all apartments. There will be a miner maintenance fee to cover snow removal, landscaping and yearly maintenance and repairs. The days of living in slum areas will be put in our past. This project is the first but it will not be our last. We intend to build as many of these communities as humanly possible."

Mr. Rollin asks, "Why such elaborate apartments, why such luxury for low-income and middle-income families?"

"Mr. Rollins "Karlon says, "this is just the type of thinking that we are trying to change, 1 this should be the norm not abnormal, this is just a clean and healthy lifestyle. And should not be considered luxury it should be considered the norm, many rich white people live like this as a normal lifestyle. I want our contributors and the community volunteers to realize what we are helping to change here.

Let's help our people have a sense of pride as to where they live. Give them a reason to do better. By putting them down you help keep them down, we are trying to lift them up to stay up.

"Well again Mr. Brooks," says Mr. Rollins, "I will say that I am impressed with what the TNBC is doing, and I wish you much success."

Karlon, "Yes thank you mister Rollins, but before I go I would like to reiterate that we are still taking an accepting volunteers, contributions and contributors for our project, it will continue. And so will we."

The Next Step

After a couple of days Karlon speaks to the board regarding the interview.

Gentlemen I just want to get some feedback on the interview myself and John just did with CNN.

"Hey Karlon, this is Jim, I think most of us feel positive about the interview. You guys represented us well, and I think the explanations of what we are doing was well understood by the audience. If everybody feels that way I think the next step for us is to decide the next step. If our finances are covered for this project, I think we should start investigating what areas would be good for the next project. I don't want there to be any gaps in our progress, I want people to feel that we are here for good and not just one hit wonders. I like the community idea. I really think we should investigate doing it again in another area, so other areas will feel we are not prioritizing our area. But we still need to keep to the funds at hand when deciding what projects to do. We just find real estate to build a couple of apartment buildings or build some community centers in additional communities or just refurbish and rebuild some buildings. With the amount of apartments, garden apartments we are building, that's going to be hard to top.

"Well" Jim, Karlon says, "That's just it I don't expect it to be easy I want our people to see that we are putting our best foot forward, as I mentioned a while back of the sacrifices made by our ancestors to get us to the point we are. I want us to make good on the efforts that they put forward. This project will house approximately 1,000 families in apartments. These families will be living in comfort not slums these families will not be struggling to pay their rent. This program is set so that they can concentrate their finance on other things. So that they can concentrate their minds on other things as far as their careers are concerned. Not be worried about rats and roaches. We will keep our money in the community, even the ShopRite and Walmart are businesses that are black owned. The city has agreed to hire more policemen and sanitation workers to cover the new neighborhood. Bus routes will be modified to cover the new area. So in doing that we have created more jobs.

Near the end or at the end of this project we will announce the next area for a new community. We are determined to keep going. Our ancestors have struggled and sacrificed their lives so that we can be in this position to do the things we are doing today. And with that I will say that I am proud of all the people that have sacrificed for this project and the progress we are making. An article has been written and it's being published by

The Newark Star Ledger. It also seems as if that same article is being published by the nationally recognized USA Today newspaper. So it seems that we have accomplished what the name national community has done to our organization being recognized nationally. I can't say enough about how we have changed the look on the face of our critics by helping one another to succeed rather than killing one another and bringing each other down. We have to strive to better ourselves and our neighbors by sacrificing as our ancestors have done. And I do not see us changing. It has already been decided that we will go back to doing projects in each city. Some cities will build schools and some cities will be apartment buildings, not too tall but just enough to house a good amount of people in the neighborhood, so that there is less homeless situations. Our new schools will not be outclassed by the schools in white neighborhoods, we will have fully equipped classrooms and modern technology in order to help teach lessons in an up-to-date manner. With the hope that this progress will continue, we have shown that we can work together and sacrifice for the good of one another and the future of our people. Our children will reap the benefits of our sacrifices and hopefully they will not only lead better lives but they will continue the progress and sacrifices we made.

Ok guys we've covered the interview now I need to remind you of my wedding coming up next week. My future wife has been working hard to make things nice. You all have a seat waiting for you, it's a small wedding party just me, my best man who is my brother. And my singing group will serve as groomsmen. So no one is offended they are not the best man. We will have a nice time at the wedding and reception, and then me and wifey are off to Hawaii for a week then back to work. But for now we still have work to do to complete this project, I am looking forward to the grand opening. We will make a big to-do about it, so that there is much publicity on it." Karlon decides to make some phone calls regarding the grand opening.

"Hello this is Karlon Brooks, I'm looking for Miss Debra Fisher

"Yes, this is Debra Fisher,"

Karlon "Yes Miss Fisher I'm calling regarding your approval for an apartment in the new complex."

"Yes I'm aware" Ms. Fisher says, "and I'm very glad and thankful that I've been approved for this apartment."

"Well Miss Fisher" Karlon says, "I would like to know if you would like to be part of the grand opening festivities? All we would like you to do is the part of cutting the ribbon and maybe say a few words which is optional. You will be representing one of the first families assigned an apartment that has been on the waiting list for City and Section 8 approval."

"Well that sounds nice" Ms. Fisher, says "I believe I would be honored to be a part of that. What do I need to do?"

"Not much," Karlon answers. "I will call you a couple of days before the festivities are to commence and you just need to be there oh, I know you have a daughter, she can be on stage with you. If you wish."

Debra, "Thank you Mr. Brooks I will wait for your call, goodbye."

Karlon steps up out of his office and goes to the desk of his sister Karien Brooks and says, "Miss Fisher is in, she will be there on stage with her daughter. so just wanted to let you know to count her in. I am going to make more calls so just to let you know."

Karlon now calls one of the construction workers.

"Hello I'm looking for Mr. Jeffries my name is Karlon Brooks."

Yes this is Mr. Jeffries."

Karlon "I'm calling to invite you to be a part of the grand opening festivities by representing the construction workers in the cutting of the ribbon."

Mr. Jeffries replies, "Wow you want me to cut the ribbon?"

Karlon says," you will not be the only one. There will be people from each part of the project on stage to cut the ribbon. "Karlon again goes to Karien.

Karlon "Oh I got another person for the festivities a construction worker by the name of Ross Jeffries who is in for participating. I will still make a few calls I'll let you in on the rest of the information tomorrow."

Karien replies, "Hey am I going to be cutting the ribbon? I can represent administrative part of the project.

Karlon's response" that's fine, Samara has enough on her plate right now so I'm not going to bother her with it." Karlon takes time to make more phone calls. This time to Mr.Lee.

"Hello Lee," Karlon says"

Yes this is Lee what's up Karlon?"

Karlon," I'm putting in order some names to cut the ribbon at the grand opening of the community festivities. I'm hoping you can be on stage with a pair of scissors in your hand."

Lee replies, "Yeah, I see the schedule of your festivities and I will not be in town during that time. However I am very glad and proud the community project is a success. Maybe you don't even realize how hard you have worked on this project. I am also happy that you reached out for help when you needed it that's a good sign a successful businessman. Karlon replies, "Who you calling a businessman?" he says with a laugh. Karlon," I wanted to have at least one member of the board on stage for the festivities.

Lee replies, "Actually you don't need that, I'm pretty sure all the board members would be satisfied with just an honorable mention.

"Yeah I understand that" Karlon replies, "I will feel more comfortable and the crowd and the community would be more hyped up with a celebrity on stage behind us or with us I should say. I know of one local pro super bowl-winning football player I can turn to if I'm in dire straits."

Lee replies," Will there be any media coverage of this event?

Karlon says, "Yeah at least one local station said they will be there. I believe there will be more. I believe CNN will come to film for future news reports.

Lee replies, "Fine I will try to pick it up and record it somehow. I will let you go to finish your roster, I will call you as soon as I am back in town, and maybe you can give me a grand tour of the place?"

Karlon says, "Yeah that's fine just let me know when you're back. I'll talk to you later bye. Karlon decides to call it a day and go home and relax. As he gets home he relaxers with Samira to go over the day.

Karlon "It looks like I have filled out the roster for people on stage cutting the ribbon, your future sister-in-law Karen wants to have a pair of scissors in her hands believe it or not. I told her you were too busy with other things to be bothered with that.

Samira replies, "Yeah, that's just part of it but I don't want to be on stage with all those people. I like it when it's just me and you talkin to someone. But yeah I'm glad you got that. It's just another "T" crossed.

Karlon turns to ask Samira, "So how are things going with the wedding plans is there anything I need to know?"

Samira replies, "Well, there will be a dress rehearsal this Saturday as a matter of fact so make plans to be there. Although it's called a dress rehearsal I'm not getting dressed it's just the last rehearsal before next Saturday. And pick up your tux on Thursday do not wait for Friday to pick it up."

Karlon "Okay baby you look like you got it all figured out so I'm in."

She turns around and looks at him and they both laugh. Two minutes later Samira turns to look at him and he is asleep.

Well it's that day, grand opening for the community. Sunday late afternoon, Karlon timed this so people would still go to church and attend the grand opening on time. With one street block blocked off at a parking lot across from the gate to the entrance of the community.

This gate is temporarily there for this event. There is a podium and seats for attendance. With a big sign on the gate Grand Opening National Black Community. The seats are filled and now the Mayor comes to the microphone.

Mayor, "Good afternoon ladies and gentlemen I am here on a proud day for our city. We have been blessed to come in an alliance with the National Black Community. This is a first in our nation. Were people of the community physically built the community, through volunteers and hard work. People that wanted this project to work. Let me repeat not just one house but the whole community. "As he says this a round of applause begins to rumble.

Mayor, "This is something you all can be proud of. We have people here on stage In all parts of this project, we have buses here to take you on a tour of the community. There are three buses that will make 3 tours each. Let me first introduce you to a young lady. On the waiting list to move into housing for the longest time. Ms. Debra Fisher. Applause for Miss Fisher as she comes to the stage.

"Hello, my name is Debra Fisher and I am proud to be one of the first families moving in to the community. And yes I have been told that I have been on the waiting list for Section 8 and City housing for the longest amount of time. I don't have much to say I just want to thank the Mayor and Mr. Brooks for treating me so well and giving me this opportunity for such nice housing." Now she turns and gives the mic back to the mayor.

Mayor, "Well as we don't have an official Master of Ceremonies I guess I am it. Now I will introduce to you one of our volunteer construction workers volunteering his physical time to help build this community,

Mr. Jeffries says, "I also don't have much to say but after looking at the completed work of the community I am so proud that I have been a part of it. I personally was not out to get an apartment but I did get enough experience to get me a job as a construction worker." Mr. Jeffries also turns and gives the microphone to the mayor.

Mayor, "Now for one of the administrative workers."

Karien, "Hello most of those that have called about housing have spoken with me, my name is Karien Brooks, I am so proud to be a part of this project and to see so many people get decent housing that has not been affordable to them in the past. National Black Community is not ending we will be here for you, I will continue to be here to help this community in any way that I can.

The mayor takes the mic and says, I now would like to introduce to you a member of the board, the financial backing of this project, he is already a success story. A member of your New York Giants Super Bowl winning team, Mr. Antonio Pierce. Again a loud applause begins.

Antonio, "Ladies and gentlemen I am not just proud to be here, but I am happy. Happy to see what has been done, we on the board administer the money by making decisions, but we don't often see the finished project. I also want to say that there has been money volunteered by Athletes and celebrities. But I really feel that you as a community should be very proud of the money that you have volunteered, without this money to the community this project would not have been done. Again after this a large applause begins to rumble. I now would like to introduce a part of the Black Community that this project could not have done without, and actually this <u>is</u> my <u>man so don't nobody m</u>ess with him Mr. Karlon Brooks. Again a large roll of applause begins. Karlon "Ladies and gentlemen, don't stop clapping, just turn to your neighbor, and continue, because that's who you're clapping for. When I say you are the ones that deserve applause, I mean you. Mr. Jeffries did not come from south jersey to make some money and go back home. He came from this community. As a matter of fact he's standing next to you. There are plenty Mr. Jeffries out there. By a show of hands any one that volunteered to this project please raise your hand" a blanket of silence filled the area as it seemed that everyone raised their hand. Karlon, "That's what I mean you did this and you should be damn proud of it. Ms. Fisher did not sneak in the back door, or come from south jersey. She lives right next door to you. And when we say she was on the waiting list the longest we mean just that. There is no one moving in this community that has been on the list longer than ms. Fisher. Being fair is the top priority of the national black community. Applause begins again. Many of you probably don't know how all of this got started. It all started when I started a website to help the local merchants communicate with each other. They are now able to know what services and products other merchants are selling. By doing this they are able to help keep our money in our community. That website is still running and part of the fabric of the community by helping the local merchants." As he says this again of roar of Applause again

"Many of you may not know that The National Black Community is just that, it's National. There are black community centers in other states and cities across our country. With the priority of helping and being fair to our people. And by the way, when we got to a million members we stopped counting," again a roar of applause begins, and chants of T N B C filled the air.

Karlon continues, "It should not go unnoticed that we got huge contributions from our black celebrities and pro sports stars, such as Mr. Antonio Pierce. And just to name a few more, Michael Strahan, Carl Banks, Mr. Ray Lewis, and Ed Reed. Mr. Michael Bennett also Mr. Curtis Granderson one of our favorite movie producers Mr. Lee and Mr. Charles S. Dutton, Mister Sean Puffy Combs, the Hollerand

Brothers real estate agency, and National Black Bank of New Jersey. Shaquille O'Neal, Charles Barkley, Patrick Ewing, and Michael Jordan. as I said this is just to name a few there are plenty more contributors such as black lawyers and judges that want to give back to the community. And just so you know, this money is not a one-time deal, some of this money is a continuing endeavor from some of these celebrities and athletes. I just wanted to give you an idea of the kind of support we have. And we will continue to build a better life for our people, so I challenge you to continue to volunteer your time to help our youth, our seniors and all that are in need until we have overcome." The loudest cheer of the day began and chants of we shall overcome began as people started loading the buses for the tour. Karlon steps back to set down and leans over and actually cries a little,

Karien comes over puts her hand on his back and says, you put your heart into that huh?.

He replies "Yes it was something heartfelt, something I had to get out. Then Karlon looks up at her and says," you think that was something? Wait till you see me at the wedding in 5 more days."

And 5 days pass in the blink of an eye, and Karlon sees himself standing in front of the church watching a dream come true. About to marry the woman he felt was custom made for him. The perfect part of this is that she feels the same way about him. Many people always compliment how they work together. All family and friends say this is a marriage meant to be. Up front with Samira is her maid of honor Maxine, and two other girlfriends, Linda and Lilly. Alongside Karlon is none other than the Devastations, Herb, Kelvin, and Victor a little noise begins as people begin to notice Mr. Lee and Mr. Peirce come into the church. And are ushered to an up front seat. The wedding goes just as beautiful as imagined. But what was not imagined was, just as the preacher said "you may kiss the bride" a cloud of smoke came up from the floor. A murmur filled the room, Karien turns to her friend and says, I knew it, I knew it, Karlon was not going to let this be a normal wedding. Something just had to happen, it just had to. So the cloud got real thick you could not see your neighbor. Music began to play, people began to whisper, it's a Luther Vandross song," Here and Now". Now as the smoke began to clear people could see the group and Karlon had turned to face the audience, standing in front of the church. The group began to sing background vocals to the song, Karlon picks up a mic and began to talk, but he is talking the lyrics to the song instead of singing. He is also explaining the words to the song as to how he feels about Samira, a lot of women began to say this is very sexy because Karlon has a very smooth sexy voice. After the song is finished Karlon and Samira kiss again and pose for a few more pictures. Now they get to the front door and the couple come out of the church and stand at the top of the stairs on their way to the limo. The street and sidewalks were filled with people, as far as you can see chanting T N B C!!! T N B C!!! T N B C!!! Karlon and Samira look at each other and kiss, then dash into the limo.

About the Author

Karlon Brooks born and raised in Newark, NJ. The natural father of Karlon Taylor Brooks and Marlin Brooks. Karlon also raised four step children. Married two times and divorced two times. Now with the love of his life, Samira Benzaid (a highschool mate). A hardworking man that finally found his niche as a Chemical Operator for a chemical Company. Being struck by cancer two times,and the second time Karlon lost the use of his legs due to a tumour being removed from his spine. This is what gave Karlon that time to write a book, but the inspiration came from the idea that black mega million sports stars actors and such can contribute to many projects needed in the black community compounded by the notion that blacks don't work together. So Karlon's vision is to show in the book just how this can be done.